School of Applied Arts
English as a 2nd Language
ALGONQUIN COLLEGE

Please Write

A Beginning Composition Text for Students of ESL

Patricia Ackert

Illustrated by Patricia Phelan Eisenberg

DISCARD

PRENTICE HALL REGENTS, Englewood Cliffs, NJ 07632

Editorial/production supervision and
interior design: Lisa A. Domínguez
Cover design: Ben Santora
Manufacturing buyer: Harry P. Baisley

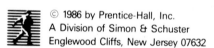 © 1986 by Prentice-Hall, Inc.
A Division of Simon & Schuster
Englewood Cliffs, New Jersey 07632

All rights reserved. No part of this book may be
reproduced, in any form or by any means,
without permission in writing from the publisher.

Printed in the United States of America

10   9

0-13-683418-3   01

Prentice-Hall International (UK) Limited, *London*
Prentice-Hall of Australia Pty. Limited, *Sydney*
Prentice-Hall Canada Inc., *Toronto*
Prentice-Hall Hispanoamericana, S.A., *Mexico*
Prentice-Hall of India Private Limited, *New Delhi*
Prentice-Hall of Japan, Inc., *Tokyo*
Simon & Schuster Asia Pte. Ltd., *Singapore*
Editora Prentice-Hall do Brasil, Ltda., *Rio de Janeiro*

Acknowledgments

I would like to thank Julia Braithwaite, Christine Gorder, Eileen Grant, and Phyllis Jae for teaching these lessons and making many valuable suggestions. Dean Jensen was also helpful with ideas. Melinda Curry typed the manuscript and made helpful suggestions.

Contents

Myself

A. Look at the model composition on page xiv. Look at the form of the composition.

B. Think about these questions:

What kind of person are you?
What do you look like?
What do you like to do?

C. Write a paragraph about yourself. Use your name as the title. Indent. Skip lines. Leave a margin at each side of the paper.

Use these questions to help you write.

1. What is your name?
2. How old are you?
3. Where are you from? (city and country)
4. What language(s) do you speak?

5. What do you look like?
6. What do you like to do in your free time?

Use some of these words and ideas:

short	slender	curly	blond
tall	a little heavy	wavy	brown
thin	hair	straight	blue
	eyes	black	

D. Check your paper.

1. Do you have a title?
2. Do you have a margin at each side of the paper?
3. Did you indent?
4. Did you skip lines?
5. Did you start each sentence with a capital letter?
6. Did you end each sentence with a period?

Lesson 2

An Interview

PRACTICE

A. Verbs

Add *-s* to the verb to form the third person singular of the present tense (the *-s* form).

I *like* to play volleyball.
She *likes* to play volleyball.

We *play* tennis every Sunday.
Tom *plays* tennis every Sunday.

B. Irregular verbs: be, have

be (am, is, are)
    I *am* from Venezuela.

He *is* from Canada.

have, has
    I *have* curly brown hair.

She *has* short blond hair.

3

B1. **Write the correct form of the verb in the blank.**

1. (speak)   They _____ Japanese.
2. (have)   Tom _____ curly brown hair.
3. (be)   I _____ tall and thin.
4. (like)   She _____ to swim.
5. (be)   His eyes _____ brown.
6. (have)   I _____ long brown hair.
7. (smile)   Betty _____ a lot.
8. (be)   I _____ twenty years old.
9. (be)   She _____ from Paris, France.
10. (be)   He _____ short.

B2.   **Write five sentences. Use these verbs: *is, has, speaks, eats, works.*

C.   **To be _____ years old**

Use the verb *be* with *years old*.

She *is* twenty-one years old.   I *am* twenty-five years old.

C1.   **Fill in the blanks.**

1. He _____ nineteen years old.
2. Mr. and Mrs. Baker are both forty-one _____ _____.
3. She _____ twenty-one years old.
4. I _____ twenty-five years old.
5. Judy _____ thirty _____ _____.

C2.   **Write two sentences. Use *years old* in each sentence.

D.   **Like to + simple verb (*like to + SV*)**

I like *to* play tennis.

D1.   **Fill in the blanks.**

1. Do you like _____ swim?
2. We _____ _____ dance.
3. I _____ _____ play baseball.

4. They _____.

5. I _____.

D2. **Write two sentences. Use *like to* **in each sentence.**

E. Capital letters

Use a capital letter for:

1. The first word in a sentence (He likes to play soccer.)
2. The name of a person (Helen, David, Mary)
3. A nationality or language (Mexican, Canadian, Spanish, English)
4. The name of a day or month (Sunday, Wednesday, August, October)
5. The names of seasons do NOT begin with a capital letter (spring, summer, fall, winter)

E1. **Put capital letters where they are necessary.**

1. I saw bob and alice at the basketball game on saturday.

2. masa speaks japanese.

3. marie is french.

4. arabs speak arabic and mexicans speak spanish.

5. january is in the winter and october is in the fall.

6. classes start on the third monday in september.

E2. **Write three sentences. Use words with capital letters from the rules in E.

F. Word order

Put these adjectives in this order. (Do not use *and* with these adjectives.)

long	straight	brown	hair
short	wavy	black	
	curly	blond	
		red	
		gray	

He has *short brown hair.*
She has *long wavy black hair.*

F1. **Write two sentences about someone's hair. Use two adjectives in the first sentences. Use three adjectives in the second sentence.

<u>WRITE</u>

A. Choose a student in the class. Ask her/him these questions. Make notes by the questions.

1. What is your name?

2. Where are you from? (city and country)

3. What language do you speak?

4. What do you like to do in your free time?

B. Describe the person. Make notes. Use some of these words and ideas:

tall	straight	black	smile
short	wavy	brown	laugh
slender	curly	blue	happy
a little heavy	long	dark	serious
hair	short	eyes	pleasant
			nice

C. Read *Check Your Paper,* on the inside front cover, numbers 1–10.

D. Now write a paragraph about this person. Use the person's name as the title. Use the person's name in the first sentence. Use the *-s* form of the verb.

Example:

Ann Baker

Ann Baker is in my class. XXXXXXXXXX
XXXXXXXXXXXXXXXX.

E. Check your paper. Use the list on the inside front cover. Use numbers 1–10.

A Person I Like

PRACTICE

A. **Review**

Fill in the blanks with verbs.

1. My mother _____ forty-five years old.
2. She _____ to cook.
3. My brother _____ blue eyes.
4. My father _____ for the government.
5. My friend _____ usually happy.

B. Subject + verb

Every sentence must have a subject (S) and a verb (V).

   S   **V**
Dan has blue eyes.

   S   **V**
She is twenty years old.

B1. Write *S* over each subject and write *V* over each verb.

1. My mother works for a large company.
2. She is a secretary.
3. My brother is short and thin.
4. Betty lives in Mexico City.
5. Everybody likes my sister.
6. She is always nice to everyone.

C. Never connect two sentences with a comma.

WRONG: ~~She is short, she has black~~ hair.

RIGHT: She is short. She has black hair.

WRONG: ~~David is from Mexico, he speaks~~ Spanish.

RIGHT: David is from Mexico and he speaks Spanish.

C1. Make each sentence correct. Use *and* in some sentences. Divide some of them into two sentences.

1. she is short she has blond hair
2. ann likes to play tennis she is a good player
3. tom likes to play soccer he also likes to read
4. he is tall he has black curly hair
5. paulo is from brazil he speaks portuguese

C2. Make each sentence correct.

1. Keiko likes to dance she is a good dancer
2. she is tall she has short black hair
3. he is from Saudi Arabia he speaks Arabic

D. Prepositions with time expressions

Use *at* with exact time.   *at* 12:00
                             at 6:30
                             at 7:14

Learn these:

in the morning   *at* night
in the afternoon   *at* noon
in the evening   *at* midnight

D1.   Put the correct preposition in each blank.

1. I usually get up _____ 7:00 _____ the morning.
2. She has classes _____ the afternoon.
3. There are also some classes _____ night.
4. Tom goes to bed _____ 11:00 _____ night.
5. What do you usually do _____ the evening?
6. Do you eat lunch _____ noon or later _____ the afternoon?
7. Mother usually goes to bed _____ midnight.

**D2.   Write six sentences. Use some of the time expressions in D.

E. An introductory sentence

A good composition has an introductory sentence. The introductory sentence introduces the composition to the reader. It is a sentence about the general idea of the composition.

Example:

MY CAR

I have a Honda Civic car. It is white with a blue interior. It is small but very comfortable. It is easy to drive and it does not use very much gas. I am glad I have this kind of car.

E1.   Now look at the model paragraph on page xiv. Read the introductory sentence.

F. A concluding sentence

> A good paragraph also has a concluding sentence to finish it. "Conclude" means "finish." What is the concluding sentence in the paragraph about my car? What is the concluding sentence in the model composition? You should write an introductory sentence and a concluding sentence in all your compositions.

WRITE

A. Write a composition about someone you know. Maybe it is your mother, father, sister, or brother. Maybe it is a friend. Write about only one person. Use the person's name for the title. Put the person's name in the introductory sentence. Read numbers 1–13 of *Check Your Paper* on the inside front cover before you begin.

> Use these ideas:
>
> 1. What does the person look like?
> 2. What kind of person is he/she?
> 3. How old is he/she?
> 4. What does he/she like to do?

B. Check your paper. Use numbers 1–13 on the inside front cover.

My Daily Activities

PRACTICE

A. **Titles**

Every composition has a title (name).

Most words in titles have capital letters.

Rules:

1. Always use a capital letter on the first word of a title.
2. Use a capital letter on all the important words.
3. *Do not* use a capital letter on
    a. prepositions (*in, on, of, for, at, between, after*)
    b. connecting words (*and, but, or*)
    c. articles (*a, an, the*)
4. *Do not* put a period at the end of a title.

A1.   Add capital letters to these titles.

1.   my classroom
2.   an important holiday
3.   between two friends
4.   busy but happy
5.   an evening at a rock concert
6.   a trip to the moon
7.   composition for foreign students
8.   life among the indians
9.   the story of my life
10.   cars and trucks

B.   Present tense

Use the present tense to describe a habitual or repeated action (something you always or usually do). Use it also to give general information.

I usually *get up* at 7:00 in the morning.
He often *plays* soccer on Sunday.
I *visit* my family every vacation.
Tom *is* a student.
I *like* to watch television.
The Earth *is* round.

Use the *-s* form of the verb with all singular subjects except *I* and *you*. This is very important. *Don't forget it!*
Be is irregular: *is*
Have is irregular: *has*

Bill usually *gets up* early.
He *has* a big breakfast.
Mary *leaves* for the university at 7:30 a.m.
She *arrives* at the university at 8:00.
My cat *is* brown.
It *likes* to sleep a lot.
My car *has* a flat tire.
The Student Union *opens* at 7:00 a.m.

Use the simple form of the verb with *I, you,* and all plural subjects.
Be is irregular: *am/are*

They never *come* to class late.
Mr. and Mrs. Baker *leave* for home at 5:00 p.m.
The students *practice* their English between classes.
You *are* all good students.
I usually *have* lunch in the cafeteria.
You *are* a good student.

7. Do you _____ television in the evening?

8. Bob never goes to the _____ in the afternoon.

**E2. Write three sentences. Use three of the expressions in E.

F. Connecting ideas

Use these words to connect ideas in a composition.

Next   After that   Then   and then

Begin a sentence with *Then, Next,* or *After that.* Use a capital letter. Use *and than* to connect two sentences into one sentence. Do not use a capital letter on *and then.*

Example:

I usually start to study at 4:00. I get my books, notebook, and pencil. *Then* I put them all on my desk. I look at my assignment notes, *and then* I find the right page. *Next* I read the directions carefully. *After that* I take a sheet of paper and put my name on it. *Then* I start to do my homework.

F1. Write *Then, and then,* or *After that* in the blanks.

1. I get up _____ I take a shower.

2. I get up. _____ I take a shower.

3. I read the directions. _____ I do the exercise.

4. I read the directions _____ I do the exercise.

5. We hand in our homework. _____ we start the new lesson.

6. We hand in our homework _____ we start the new lesson.

7. They eat dinner _____ they wash the dishes.

8. They eat dinner. _____ they wash the dishes.

**F2. Write four pairs of sentences. Use *Next, After that, Then, and then.*

WRITE

Think about this question:

What are your daily activities? (What do you usually do every day?)

A. Write a composition about your daily activities. Use the present tense. Write a title and indent. Leave margins at the sides of the paper. Write an introductory sentence and a concluding sentence. Use some of these words and ideas:

get up	tea	leave for the university	watch television
take a shower	toast	have lunch	talk with my friends
comb my hair	rice	take a nap	study
get dressed	eggs	rest	do my homework
have breakfast	cereal	relax	have dinner
coffee	brush my teeth	play soccer	wash the dishes
			go to bed

Use other words and ideas too.

Also use some of these connecting words in a few sentences:

Then   After that   Next   and then

B. Check your paper. Use number 5–14 on the inside front cover.

My Home

PRACTICE

A. **Review**

Write a good introductory sentence for each title.

1. An Important Holiday
2. My Favorite Sport
3. My Baby Sister
4. Life in Japan
5. My Friend David

B.   There is/there are

Use a singular noun ofter *there is*. Then use *it* in the second sentence.

There is a small *garden* behind my house. *It* has flowers and vegetables.

Use a plural noun after *there are*. Then use *they* in the second sentence.

There are three *bedrooms* in my house. *They* are on the second floor.

B1.   Look at the noun after the blank. Is it singular or plural? Write *there is* or *there are* in the first blank. Write *it* or *they* in the second blank.

1. _____ a blue sofa in the living room. _____ is near the window.

2. _____ flowers and vegetables in the garden. _____ do not grow during the winter.

3. _____ chairs and a table in the dining room. _____ are made of wood.

4. At the side of the house _____ a garage. _____ has space for two cars.

5. Behind the house _____ a swimming pool.

6. _____ a television in the living room.

7. _____ two bathrooms in the house.

8. Around the house _____ a big yard.

9. In the garage _____ two cars.

10. _____ three bedrooms on the second floor.

**B2.   Write two sentences using *there is* and two sentences using *there are*.

C.   Adjectives

An adjective describes a noun. Put an adjective before a noun.

a *large* house   a *small* garden
my *new* car   *brown* eyes

Put an adjective after *be*.

My house is *large*.   The garden is *small*.
My car is *new*.   His eyes are *brown*.

An adjective does not have a plural form.

a *large* house   a *new* car
three *large* houses   five *new* cars

C1. **Write a sentence. Put the words in the correct order. Then put a circle around the adjective.**

1. house / white / his / is
2. has / house / big / my / living room / a
3. living room / the / big / is
4. car / have / new / we / a
5. he / jeans / wears / old
6. lives / beautiful / she / a / in / house
7. is / stove / green / the

C2. **Write five sentences. Put an adjective in each sentence.

D. Direct objects

Every sentence must have a subject (S) and a verb (V). Some sentences also have a direct object (D.O.). The direct object is directly after the verb. There is nothing between the verb and the direct object. The direct object is usually a noun. Sometimes the noun has an adjective or an article (a, an, the). The direct object answers the question *"what?"* or *"who?"*.

```
S           V          D.O.
```
Jim usually has (a big sandwich) for lunch.
Jim usually has ___what?___ for lunch.   (a big sandwich)

```
S        V     D.O.
```
I often visit John on Sunday.
I often visit ___who (m)?___ on Sunday.   (John)

D1. **Write *S* over the subject, *V* over the verb, and *D.O.* over the direct object.**

1. My house has three bedrooms.
2. I often play pool in the games room.
3. She likes her baby brother very much.
4. He visits London every year.
5. She wears a sweater in cold weather.
6. Bill sometimes has some coffee in the evening.
7. They watch television every night.
8. We usually eat lunch in the cafeteria.
9. The house has a wall around it.
10. Barbara leaves the university at 4:30 every day.

D2. **Write a sentence. Put the words in the correct order. Draw a circle around the direct object.

1. baseball / play / I / Sunday / every

2. she / car / a / new / has

3. wears / class / he / jeans / to

4. home / we / at / breakfast / eat

5. window / has / the living room / big / a

6. homework / at / their / they / do / night

E. Plural nouns: spelling

1. Most plural nouns end in *-s*.

room – rooms		tree – trees
car – cars		house – houses

2. Add *-es* to a noun that ends in *s, ch, sh,* or *x*.

bus – buses		dish – dishes
church – churches		box – boxes

3. If a noun ends in *y* and there is a consonant before the *y*, change the *y* to *i* and add *-es*.

baby – babies		lady – ladies

4. If a noun ends in *y* and there is a vowel before the *y*, add *-s*.

boy – boys		day – days

5. If a noun ends in *f*, change the *f* to *v* and add *-es*. If a noun ends in *fe*, change the *f* to *v* and add *-s*.

leaf – leaves		wife – wives

6. Some nouns are irregular. Memorize them.

foot – feet		man – men
tooth – teeth		woman – women
sheep – sheep		child – children

Summary

Singular	Plural
most nouns	-s
-s -ch -sh -x	-es
consonant + y vowel + y	-ies -ys
-f -fe	-ves

E1. Write the plural form of each noun.

tax	knife	key
lunch	child	table
woman	shelf	ash
sheep	box	tooth
river	toy	man
family	library	match
dress		foot

F. One subject in a composition

A good composition is about only one subject or idea. Every sentence is about the same subject. Look at the example. The underlined sentence is not a good sentence for this paragraph because it is about a different subject. It does not belong in this composition.

Example:

I am always very busy during the week. I get up at 7:00 and leave for the university at 7:45. My university is beautiful and has modern buildings. I have classes or study until 4:00 and then I go home. I relax for a while, have dinner, and study some more. Then I watch television and go to bed. I am usually tired after a busy day.

F1. Read each paragraph. Underline the sentence that does not belong.

1. María is one of my classmates. She is from Colombia and speaks Spanish. Bogotá is the capital of Colombia. María is tall and pretty. She smiles a lot and is an excellent student.

2. My father is a businessman. Every day he has breakfast with his family and then goes to work. He has brown eyes and curly brown hair. He works in his office all morning and then usually has lunch at a restaurant. He works until 5:00 in the afternoon and then comes home. He is happy to be at home at the end of a busy day.

3. My composition class is in an old building. The classroom walls are white and the desks and chairs are brown. There are large windows in one wall. The chalkboard is in the front of the room near the door. My composition class is difficult and I do not like to write compositions. The room is cool in warm weather and warm in winter. I like my classroom.

WRITE

A. **Think about your house or apartment in your country. Is it in a city, in a small town, or in a village? In your imagination stand in front of your house and look at it. Then walk through it. Write a composition about your house.**

Use some of these words and ideas:

house	porch	outside	rooms
city	wall	around	living room
small	yard	in front of	dining room
town	trees	behind	kitchen
village	flowers	in back of	bedroom
garage	swimming pool	beside	bathroom
			furniture

B. **Use these expressions and underline them.**

1. *there is*
2. *there are*
3. two adjectives

C. **Check your paper. Use numbers 5–15.**

Did you use the expressions in B and underline them?

Lesson 6

Yesterday

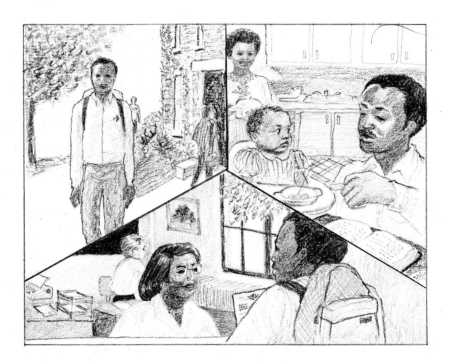

PRACTICE

A. Review

A1. Add *Then* or *and then* to each pair of sentences. Use correct punctuation.

1. I get up and take a shower. I get dressed.
2. Mary has breakfast. She leaves for work.
3. Bob has breakfast. He brushes his teeth.
4. We finish class. We go home.
5. My last class is at 1:00. I have lunch at the cafeteria.

A2.   Put the correct word in the blank.

1. I usually _____ lunch _____ 1:00.
2. I _____ my homework in the afternoon.
3. I leave _____ home after my last class.
4. Sometimes I stop at the supermarket and arrive home _____ 4:00.
5. I go _____ bed late on Saturday night.
6. Sometimes I go _____ a movie on Friday night.
7. I like _____ eat dinner at a restaurant.

A3.   Write a sentence with the words in the correct order. Then draw a line under the direct object.

1. for breakfast / has / coffee and toast / my brother
2. speaks / very well / English / she
3. spend / my vacation / at the beach / I
4. on weekends / soccer / plays / he
5. he / very well / his reading class / teaches
6. she / has / for lunch / a sandwich and coffee

B.   Past tense

Use the past tense to describe a completed action, an action that is completely finished.

I walked to class yesterday.
He lived in France from 1975 to 1980.
They were at a party last night.

Add *-ed* to regular verbs to form the past tense. If the verb ends in *-e*, just add *-d*. There is no *-s* form in the past tense.

walk	walked	live	lived
brush	brushed	use	used

Spelling

1. The rule for adding *-ed* to verbs that end in *-y* is the same as the rule for adding *-s* to nouns. If there is a consonant before the *-y*, change the *y* to *i* and add *-ed*. If there is a vowel before the *-y* just add *-ed*.
       study   studied   play   played
2. The 1-1-1 (one-one-one) rule
    If a verb has 1 syllable with 1 vowel followed by 1 consonant, double the consonant and add *-ed*.
       shop   shopped   BUT: help   helped
       plan   planned   clean   cleaned

C. Irregular verbs

Some verbs are irregular in the past tense. Learn these verb forms.

be – was, were	go – went	have – had	drive – drove
eat – ate	take – took	write – wrote	spend – spent
do – did	get – got	leave – left	buy – bought

C1. Write the past tense for each verb.

study	take	write
drop	go	plan
eat	get	have
hurry	be	talk
leave	do	attend
	stay	

C2. Fill in each blank with the past tense of a verb from C.

1. Yesterday Pat _____ up at 7:00.
2. Clara _____ a new dress last week.
3. She _____ $100 on new clothes.
4. Frank _____ for work at 6:00.
5. He _____ breakfast at the restaurant in his office building.
6. I _____ my car to class.
7. Last Sunday I _____ a letter to my parents.
8. We _____ our homework this morning.
9. She _____ a shower last night.
10. George _____ dinner at his parents' house last Saturday.
11. They _____ to a basketball game last night.
12. Sarah _____ sick yesterday.

**C3 Write four sentences in the past tense.

D. Useful expressions

Learn these:

go to class	go downtown	yesterday morning
go to school	go shopping	yesterday afternoon
go to work	go skiing	last night
	go swimming	

D1. Fill in the blanks. Some blanks do not need any word.

1. My sister went _____to_____ work _____at_____ 8:30.
2. My little brother goes _____ school every morning.
3. We went to a basketball game _____last_____ night.
4. I go _____to_____ class _____ the morning.
5. George often went _____ downtown on the bus last year.
6. _____In_____ morning Mary cleaned her apartment.
7. He likes _____ go _____to_____ shopping on Saturday.
8. I went _____ swimming every day last summer.
9. We visited one of our friends _____this_____ afternoon.

**D2. Use five of the expressions in D in sentences.

E. Count and noncount nouns

We can count some things. These are count nouns. A count noun has a plural form. It can have a number in front of it.

a building	2 buildings
a dollar	6 dollars
a room	4 rooms

We cannot count some things. These are noncount nouns. (*Non-* means *no* or *not.*) A noncount noun does not have a plural form and it cannot have a number in front of it.

air	water	fruit	toast	juice
chalk	coffee	bread	rice	homework
furniture	milk	butter	meat	money
soap	tea	cheese	food	weather

We ofter put an indefinite article (a, an) before a count noun.

a woman	an apple	a tree

Use *an* before a word that begins with a vowel *sound.*

an *apple*	an *Indian*	an *umbrella*
an *elephant*	an *old* house	an *hour*
	BUT: a (y)university	

We often put *some* before a noncount noun.

some furniture	some coffee	some soap

We often put *some* before a plural count noun too.

some chairs	some buildings	some rooms

Summary

	Count	Noncount
	singular and plural	no plural
	singular: *a, an* plural: numbers, *some*	*some*
	a banana an orange two chairs five dollars some sentences	some fruit some orange juice some furniture some money some homework

E1. Put *a* or *an* before each singular count noun. Put *some* before each noncount noun or plural count noun.

1. We live in _____ old house.
2. There is _____ fruit on the kitchen table.
3. Please put _____ bananas on the plate.
4. We need _____ fresh air in this room.
5. There is _____ chalk on the chalkboard.
6. They have _____ new furniture in their living room.
7. We need to buy _____ food at the supermarket.
8. Is there _____ orange in the refrigerator?
9. There is _____ water on the bathroom floor.
10. She has _____ new sofa and _____ new chairs.

**E2. Use these words in sentences: *apple, orange juice, chairs,* and *furniture*.

F. Combining sentences

A good composition has some short sentences and some long ones. This makes the composition more interesting. You can combine two short sentences to make one long sentence.

Method 1:

I got up. I took a shower.
I got up and took a shower.

In the afternoon he went home. In the afternoon he did his homework.
In the afternoon he went home and did his homework.

F1. Combine these sentences. Write the subject only once.

1. Tom collects stamps. Tom plays the guitar.
2. We watch television in the evening. We read in the evening.
3. She is from Venezuela. She speaks Spanish.
4. After class Ann went home. After class Ann had lunch.
5. In the morning she drives to the university. In the morning she has breakfast in the cafeteria.

**F2. Write five sentences like the ones in F. Each sentence will have one subject and two different verbs.

WRITE

A. Write a composition about what you did yesterday. Use the past tense. Write some short sentences and some long sentences. (See page 16 for some ideas.)

Write three paragraphs:

Paragraph 1   A. Introductory sentence
                      B. In the morning
Paragraph 2   A. In the afternoon
Paragraph 3   A. In the evening
                      B. Concluding sentence

B. Use these expressions and underline them:

1. four irregular verbs from page 25 C
2. two noncount nouns from page 26 E

C. Check your paper. Use numbers 8–15.

Right Now

PRACTICE

A. Review

A1. Write the correct present form of the verb.

1. (go)   Keiko _____ to the Student Union every day.
2. (visit) Tom _____ his parents every Sunday.
3. (get)   I usually _____ up at 7:00.
4. (like)   We _____ to go out on Saturday night.
5. (play)   Ann _____ tennis every Sunday afternoon.
6. (have)   Mr. and Mrs. Smith always _____ Sunday dinner at a restaurant.

7. (be)   Phil __is__ a student.
8. (finish)   After Mary __finished__ her homework, she usually
   (watch) __watch__ television.

A2.   Add punctuation and capital letters to these sentences.

1. bob likes to play soccer on the weekend he likes to go to the pool too
2. my house has seven rooms there is a garage at the side of the house
3. there is a wall around the house there are several trees and flower beds
4. my university is large there are a lot of buildings
5. I got up and took a shower then I had breakfast and left for the university

A3.   Write the plural of each noun.

class	fox	woman
loaf	secretary	life
foot	toy	brush
teacher	sheep	monkey
knife	child	girl
	beach	

B.   Present continuous (*be* + V-ing)

Use the present of *be* (am, is, are) and the *-ing* form (present participle) of another verb for the present continuous tense.

We *are studying* English now.
The teacher *is explaining* the lesson.

Use the present continuous for something that is happening right now.

I *am sitting* in class now.
My brother *is studying* in New York this year.

Spelling

1. If a verb ends in *-e*, drop the *-e* and add *-ing*.
   write – writing   leave – leaving
2. Use the 1-1-1 rule. (See page 24B.)
   shop – shopping   plan – planning
3. Do not change a verb that ends in *-y*.
   study – studying   hurry – hurrying

B1.   Write the *-ing* form of each verb.

carry	eat	do
fly	go	stop
drive	visit	lose
get	make	hurry
drink	ride	study
	drop	

B2.   Change each sentence to the present continuous. Change the time expression to *now*.

1.   My father drives to work every day.
2.   My sister does her homework in the evening.
3.   My brother rides his bike to school.
4.   My mother cooks breakfast.
5.   They have breakfast together every morning.
6.   She takes a nap in the afternoon.
7.   They drink coffee and talk.
8.   She watches television after dinner.
9.   He telephones my uncle before lunch.

**B3.   Write five sentences using the present continuous and *now*.

C.   Demonstratives

	Singular	Plural
Here	this	these
There	that	those

This student with me is from Malaysia.
These students with me are from Malaysia.

That student over there is from Kuwait.
Those students over there are from Kuwait.

C1. Write *this, that, these,* or *those* in each blank. Use capital letters if necessary.

1. _____ book in my hand is a geography book.

2. _____ men across the room are from Mexico.

3. _____ papers here on my desk are tests.

4. Is _____ woman in the next room a lawyer?

5. Do _____ people over there speak French?

6. _____ student with me is from Venezuela.

7. Who is _____ man in the street near the car?

8. _____ houses here on this street are very old.

**C2. Write four sentences. Use *this, that, these,* and *those.*

D. **The indefinite article *a, an***

Use *a/an* before a singular noun. Use *an* before a word that begins with a vowel sound.

Use *a/an* when you write or speak about a noun for the first time. *A/an* before a noun shows that a person is a member of a general class or kind of people. *A/an* shows that a place or thing is one of a general class of places or things.

Mary is *an* engineer. (Mary is one of all the engineers in the world.)
Montreal is *a* city. (It is one of the many cities in the world.)
I went to *a* party last night. (There are many parties. I went to one of them.)

Use *a/an* before a singular noun.	Montreal is *a city.*
Use *a/an* before an adjective and a noun.	Montreal is *a large city.*
Do not use *a/an* before an adjective alone.	Montreal is *large.*

Your sister is *a child.*
Your sister is *a beautiful child.*
Your sister is *beautiful.*

Do not use *a/an* before a plural noun.	*Cars* are expensive.
Do not use *a/an* before a noncount noun.	*Fruit* is good for you.

D1. Pur *a* or *an* in the blank if it is necessary.

1. New York is _____ city.

2. New York is _____ large, noisy, exciting city.

3. Last weekend I went to _____ party.

4. Gary is _____ excellent basketball player.

5. Bob usually wears _____ jeans, _____ polyester shirt, _____ heavy blue jacket, and _____ black shoes in winter. Sometimes he wears _____ boots.

6. She has _____ round face, _____ green eyes, and _____ brown hair.

7. I like _____ Mexican food but I do not like _____ American food.

8. Marie is _____ beautiful and _____ intelligent. She is _____ very friendly.

9. I would like _____ bread, _____ cheese, _____ fruit, and _____ coffee.

10. My class is in _____ old building.

11. We ate dinner at _____ restaurant last night.

D2. Write four sentences using *a* or *an*.

E. Prepositional phrases

A phrase is a group of words but it is not a sentence.

A prepositional phrase has a preposition and an object. The object is usually a noun. A prepositional phrase sometimes has an article (a, an, the) or an adjective too. (See the list of prepositions on page 159 of the grammar reference section.)

These are some prepositional phrases:

for dinner	after dinner	after my last class
in the morning	on Saturday	on Sunday afternoon

Put some prepositional phrases at the end of your sentences. Put some at the beginning. This makes the composition more interesting.

Example:

John leaves for class *at 8:00*. He has classes and studies in the library *until noon*. *In the afternoon* he has two classes. *After his last class* he goes home. He does his homework and watches television *in the evening*.

E1. Add the prepositional phrase to the sentence. Write each sentence two ways.

1. (on Sunday)   I usually go swimming.

2. (in the morning)   He cleaned his room and washed his car.

3. (on Saturday night)   We had a small party.

E2 Write three sentences with prepositional phrases. Do each sentence two ways.

WRITE

A. It is 10:00 in your country right now. What is everybody in your family doing? Write a composition about what your family is doing right now. Tell about your parents, your sisters and brothers, and your grandparents. Use the present continuous. Use this sentence for the introductory sentence: *It is 10:00 a.m. in my country right now.*

B. Check your paper using numbers 8–17.

Habitual Actions

A. Review

A1. Fill in the blanks. Some blanks do not need a word.

1. My mother gets up _____ 6:00.

2. My brother goes _____ work _____ 7:30.

3. My sister leaves _____ the university a half hour later.

4. We eat dinner together _____ the evening.

5. I _____ my homework every day.

6. We often _____ rice, meat, and coffee _____ dinner.

7. She usually eats _____ home.

8. She goes _____ home in the afternoon.

9. _____ the evening they watch _____ television, go to _____ movie, or listen _____ the radio.

10. Mother goes _____ bed early.

A2.   **Put capital letters on these titles.**

1. my best friend

2. a bad day

3. my mother's daily activities

4. sports in germany

5. the geography of china

6. life at an american university

7. under the sea

8. indian life before columbus

A3.   **Each sentence has one mistake. Find it and correct it.**

WRONG

1. I visited my aunt before two months.

2. I am thinking to going to New York.

3. I am glad I studying at this university.

4. I am looking something for you.

5. I going to New York.

6. She is going to take breakfast early tomorrow morning.

7. Tomorrow I will go to swimming.

8. This is a views of the mountains.

9. I drank some of milk because I was thirsty.

10. I had for breakfast eggs, toast, and coffee.

B.   **The negative present tense (*be* + *not*; S + *do/does* + *not* + SV)**

Put *not* after *be* to form the negative present tense.

He *is* busy.
He *is not* busy.

Put *do/does not* before the simple verb to form the negative of other verbs.

I *watch* television in the evening.
I *do not watch* television in the evening.

He *has* breakfast at home.
He *does not have* breakfast at home.

B1.   Change each sentence to the negative.

1. She gets up at 5:00 a.m.
2. I leave for work at 6:00 a.m.
3. They are at home now.
4. He listens to his car radio on the way to class.
5. She is late for class.
6. I have a hamburger for breakfast.
7. We go to work at 7:30.
8. He is at the beach today.

**B2.   Write three negative sentences in the present tense. Use *be* in one of the sentences.

C.   Time words: always, usually, often, sometimes, seldom, never (These words are adverbs of frequency).

Put these time words after the verb *be*.

She is *always* late for class.
We are *never* busy on Sunday.

Put these time words before other verbs.

I *usually* get up at 7:00 a.m.
My brother *often* goes shopping in the evening.

C1.   Add the time word to the sentence.

1. (never)   I get up at 4:30 a.m.
2. (usually)   My father leaves for work at 8:00.
3. (never)   Anna has a hamburger for breakfast.
4. (sometimes)   She has breakfast at the university.
5. (always)   We are tired after our last class.
6. (seldom)   Paul is in the library in the afternoon.
7. (often)   My sister goes to a movie in the evening.

**C2.   Write five sentences with some of the time words. Use *be* and other verbs.

D. Spelling

The rules for adding -*s* to verbs are the same as the rules for adding -*s* to nouns.

1. Add -*s* to the simple form of most verbs for the third person singular.

    eat – eats   get – gets   like – likes

2. If a verb ends in *s, ch, sh,* or *x* add -*es*.

    pass – passes   finish – finishes
    teach – teaches   box – boxes

3. If a verb ends in *y* and there is a consonant before the *y*, change the *y* to *i* and add -*es*.

    study – studies   try – tries

4. If a verb ends in *y* and there is a vowel before the *y*, just add -*s*.

    play – plays   enjoy – enjoys

5. *Do* and *go* are irregular.

    do – does   go – goes

D1. Write the -*s* form of each verb.

fly	watch	touch
miss	carry	push
study	like	get
do	wish	have
say	wash	copy
	go	

E. The definite article *the*

You can use *the* with all kinds of nouns—singular and plural, count and noncount.

1. Use *the* when both the writer and reader (or speaker and listener) are thinking about the same thing or person.

    The cafeteria is closed today.
        (the cafeteria where we always eat)
    I want to visit *the* art museum.
        (the art museum on campus)
    The teacher gave us a lot of homework today.
        (the teacher of the class we finished five minutes ago)

2. Use *the* if the noun is already identified in the sentence before.

    I had to study for *a test* last weekend.
    The test was hard.
    There are *two large tables* in our classroom.
    The tables are in the back of the room.

3. Use *the* if the noun is identified by a phrase after the noun.

    The tables *in our classroom* are large.
    The homework *for today* was easy.

4. Do not use *the* with a noun used in a general way.
    People must have *food* and *water*.
    Water is necessary for all living things.
    Susan is studying *history*.
    Peter likes *coffee*.

5. Use *the* with a general noun if a phrase identifies it.
    The people *in my class* are from five different countries.
    The water *in this glass* is warm.
    Susan is studying *the* history of *Japan*.
    Peter does not like *the* coffee *in the student cafeteria*.

E1.   Put *a, an,* or *the* in the blanks. Some blanks do not need a word.

1. I went to _____ restaurant with some friends last night. _____ restaurant is new and very nice.
2. _____ water is very important in desert countries.
3. _____ sugar is sweet.
4. Please pass me _____ sugar.
5. He has _____ class at 8:00. He leaves home early because _____ class is across campus from the bus stop.
6. I tried to call the bus station for _____ hour but _____ line was busy.
7. _____ engineering is a difficult major.
8. Most of _____ people in Arizona were born somewhere else.
9. She ate dinner and then washed _____ dishes.

**E2.   Write three sentences. Use *the* in each sentence.

F.   A list in a sentence (_____, _____, and _____)

We often write a list of three or more things in a sentence. Separate the things in the list with commas. Write *and* or *or* before the last thing in the list.

In the morning I get up, take a shower, comb my hair, and brush my teeth.
I usually have coffee, toast, and eggs for breakfast.
My parents, my sisters, and my brother all live in Toronto.

F1.   Add commas and the word in parentheses to these sentences.

1. (and)   I like to have a hamburger fries a soda for lunch.
2. (and)   Ali Mohammed Abdul are in my class.
3. (or)   In the evenings my sister watches television goes out with some friends works on her stamp collection.
4. (and)   After class I go home have some lunch take a nap.

5. (and)   Tom likes to play volleyball basketball soccer.

6. (or)   We like to go swimming play tennis have a picnic on the weekend.

7. (and)   She cleans her apartment washes her clothes goes shopping on Saturdays.

**F2. Write three sentences like the ones in F1.

WRITE

A. Write a composition about a friend, your brother, or your sister. Tell what the person does every day. Use the -s form of the verb. Use the person's name in the first sentence.

Use some of the ideas in Lesson 4, page 16.
Write three paragraphs.

Paragraph 1	A. Introductory sentence
	B. In the morning
Paragraph 2	A. In the afternoon
Paragraph 3	A. In the evening
	B. Concluding sentence

B. Use these expressions and underline them.

1. a prepositional phrase at the beginning of a sentence
2. two of these words: always, usually, sometimes, seldom, never
3. a list of three things in one sentence
4. two connecting words (Then, After that, and then, Next)

C. Check your paper. Use numbers 10–17.

A Good Day/A Bad Day

PRACTICE

A. Review

A1. Write the past tense of each verb.

eat	be	do
take	get	write
leave	have	go
buy	spend	drive

A2. **Some sentences do not belong in these paragraphs. Draw a line under them.**

1.   On weekdays I am usually busy. I get up at 7:00, take a shower, and have breakfast. Then I brush my teeth. My house has two bathrooms. I spend the morning at the university. There are 20,000 students at my university. After my last class I go home and have lunch. I relax for an hour and then I do my homework. In the evening I usually study some more and watch television. I go to bed at 11:30 because I have to get up early the next day.

2.   On weekends I enjoy myself. My parents both work on Saturday. I go shopping or spend some time at a friend's apartment. Her apartment has two bedrooms. On Saturday night I go dancing or go to a movie. Sometimes I go out for dinner. Sometimes I stay home all day Sunday and watch television or read. Then I am ready to start studying again on Monday. I am a student at the University of Michigan.

A3. **Put *a, an,* or *the* in the blanks. Some blanks do not need a word.**

1.   I was born in _____ small town in Wisconsin.
2.   Betty grew up in Chicago. Chicago is _____ large city.
3.   _____ name of my first teacher was Miss Cook.
4.   In high school I studied _____ science, _____ history, _____ English, and _____ mathematics.
5.   I studied _____ history and geography of my country.
6.   I did not study _____ English because they did not teach it at my school. _____ school was too small.
7.   _____ teachers at my school were very strict.

B. Past tense—negative (*be + not, did not +* SV)

Use *not* with the past tense of *be* for the negative form. Write *not* after *was* or *were.*

We *were not* home last weekend.
He *was not* in class yesterday.

Use *did not* with the simple verb for the negative form of the past tense of other verbs.

I *did not walk* to class yesterday.
He *did not go* to Washington last weekend because he was sick.

B1. **Change each sentence to the negative past. Change the time expression in numbers 4–6.**

1. Ruth ate breakfast this morning.

2. She went shopping yesterday afternoon.

3. Robert was at the International Student Club party last night.

4. I do not go home on the weekend.

5. David does not do his homework in the morning.

6. We do not wash our car every week.

B2. **Write four sentences using the negative past tense. Use *be* in one of the sentences.

C. Irregular verbs

Learn these verbs.

sleep – slept	send – sent	make – made	cost – cost
read – read	lend – lent	teach – taught	wake – woke
meet – met	feel – felt	begin – began	find – found

C1. **Fill in the blanks with the correct form of the irregular verbs.**

1. Yesterday I _____ a new Malaysian student.

2. The student and I _____ to talk right away.

3. I did not _____ up early this morning.

4. Alice went downtown last Saturday but she did not _____ a place to park.

5. Betty _____ happy when she saw her grade.

6. I am tired this morning because I did not _____ very well last night.

7. Phil bought a birthday card and _____ it to his sister.

8. The card _____ $1.00.

9. I _____ a cake yesterday.

10. The teacher _____ the students some irregular verbs last week.

11. She _____ the newspaper this morning.

12. Victor _____ his pencil to Marie.

C2. **Use the past tense of six of the irregular verbs in sentences.

D. Possessives

Subject Pronouns		Possessive Adjectives *(with a noun)*	
I	we	my	our
you	you	your	your
he		his	
she	they	her	their
it		its	

Use possessive adjectives with a noun.

His family lives in Caracas.
Her mother works for a large company.

Possessives have the same form with a singular or plural noun.

My shirt is in the closet.
My shirts are in the closet.
Their car is old.
Their cars are old.

D1.   Put the right possessive form in the blank.

1. (I) _____ favorite subject in school was mathematics.
2. (They) _____ house is on a quiet street.
3. (We) _____ team won most of the games last year.
4. The cat caught (it) _____ tail in the door.
5. (She) _____ parents are both doctors.
6. Does (you) _____ family live in Paris?
7. (He) _____ father is an engineer.

**D2.   Use four of the possessive adjectives in sentences.

E. Prepositions: at

Use *at* to show place (location).

Please meet me *at* the Student Union at 6:00.
She had dinner *at* a restaurant last night.
She arrived *at* the university at 7:45.

Use *at* in some time expressions too.

at 6:00   *at* night   *at* noon   *at* midnight

E1. Write *at*, *in*, or *to* in the blanks.

1. I usually buy my food _____ a supermarket.
2. She did not arrive _____ the university until 9:00.
3. I arrived late _____ night but my brother met me _____ the airport.
4. Do you like to go _____ the movies?
5. We were _____ the beach all day yesterday.
6. Sometimes they drive _____ the coast for their vacation.
7. What time did you go _____ bed last night?
8. We had a big party _____ my apartment Saturday.
9. My little brother was _____ school all day and _____ home _____ the evening.

**E2. Use *at* in three sentences.

F. Sentence combining: but (S + V + *but* + S + V)

Each part of the sentence must have a subject and a verb.

Method 2

I tried to call you last night. The line was busy.
I tried to call you last night but the line was busy.
We wanted to eat at the student cafeteria. It was closed.
We wanted to eat at the student cafeteria but it was closed.

F1. Combine these sentences using *but*.

1. I wanted to leave early. I could not start my car.
2. He expected to get a poor grade on the quiz. He passed it.
3. Paul felt sick this morning. He decided to go to class anyway.
4. Ann planned to visit the art museum. She was too busy.

**F2. Write four sentences using *but*. Use the past tense of some irregular verbs.

WRITE

A. Think about a day in your life that was very good or very bad. Write a composition about that day.

B. Use these expressions and underline them.

        1. a sentence with *but*

        2. two irregular verbs

        3. a negative sentence

C. Check your paper using numbers 10–17.

Two People

PRACTICE

A. Review

A1. **Add capital letters where they are necessary.**

1. my brother's wife is french.
2. carol is studying german but her brother is studying spanish.
3. my best friend is venezuelan.
4. yesterday was tuesday.
5. I was born in april.
6. february is in the winter.

A2. **Write the -*s* form (third person singular) of each verb.**

pass	cry	catch
hurry	do	marry
teach	have	go
ask	put	pray
enjoy	wash	look
	copy	

A3. **Each sentence has one mistake. Correct it.**

WRONG

1. We met Edmundo, he is from Chile.
2. At 1:00 we had lunch then we played football.
3. I went to shopping in the morning.
4. I had a breakfast early yesterday morning.
5. She gets up and then take a shower.
6. When finishes her assignment she usually watches television.
7. He had for lunch a sandwich, milk, and fruit.
8. She likes to cooks.
9. He is doctor.
10. He does not like the sports.

B. **Comparisons (adj. + -*er* + than, more . . . than, good – better, bad – worse)**

We use adjectives to compare two people or things.

1. When an adjective has one syllable, add -*er* and use *than*.
    Ann is *taller than* Paula.
    My car is *older than* yours.
2. When an adjective has two syllables and ends in -*y*, add -*er* and use *than*.
    Spanish is *easier than* French.
    Sarah is *prettier than* Marie.
3. Spelling: Use the *y* rule and the 1-1-1 rule before -*er*.
    busy – busier   big – bigger
4. Use *more than* with adjectives that have three or more syllables.
    Houses are usually *more expensive than* apartments.
    Tony is *more intelligent than* Frank.
5. *Good* and *bad* are irregular.
    Chocolate ice cream is *good* but
    strawberry ice cream is *better*.
    Tom is a *bad* student.
    Peter is a *worse* student *than* Tom.

B1. **Write the comparison form of these adjectives. Use *than*.**

tall	interesting
easy	difficult
intelligent	fat
thin	pretty
bad	good

B2. **Write the correct comparison form in the blank.**

1. (old)   Ruth is _____ Carol.

2. (bad)   The weather is _____ today _____ it was yesterday.

3. (young)   My brother is _____ my sister.

4. (busy)   A secretary is _____ a receptionist.

5. (happy)   I am usually _____ on Friday afternoon _____ on Monday morning.

6. (good)   Sue is a _____ tennis player _____ David.

7. (easy)   Typing is _____ to read _____ handwriting.

8. (delicious)   Ice cream is _____ milk.

9. (beautiful)   San Francisco is _____ Los Angeles.

10. (nice)   Spring is _____ winter.

B3. **Write five sentences using a comparison.

C.   some/any

Use *some* with affirmative statements. Use *any* with negative statements. Use both *some* and *any* with questions.

Do you have *some* French stamps in your collection?
Do you have *any* French stamps in your collection?
My older brother has *some* French stamps but I do *not* have *any*.

Use a plural or noncount noun after *any*.

She does not have any blue *dresses*.
I did not see any nice *furniture* at the department store.
Do you have some *money*?
We did not see any *elephants* at the zoo.

C1. Write *some* or *any* in the blanks.

1. My younger sister does not play _____ musical instruments.
2. _____ people make friends easily.
3. Do you have _____ friends from Quebec?
4. I cannot lend you _____ money because I have just enough to pay for my lunch.
5. Dan took _____ friends to the science museum.
6. Did you get _____ mail this morning?
7. Did Paul buy _____ new clothes for his summer vacation?
8. She did not forget _____ of the new words.

**C2. Write two questions and two statements using *some* and *any*.

D. Prepositions: to

Use *to* to show movement.

My sister goes *to* work at 8:00 a.m.
I walked *to* the bus stop.

D1. Put *to, in,* or *at* in the blanks.

1. I want to go _____ the movies tomorrow.
2. There is a good movie _____ the new theater.
3. What time do you come _____ class?
4. I have to go _____ the drugstore.
5. Did you go _____ the basketball game last night?
6. She grew up _____ the mountains.
7. I usually drive _____ the university.
8. We usually meet _____ the bus stop _____ 2:30.
9. Did you walk _____ the stadium?
10. I eat lunch _____ 2:00 _____ the afternoon.

**D2. Write three sentences using *to* to show movement.

E. Combining sentences: and . . . too, and . . . either, but

Method 3a   and . . . too

Gina is from Italy. Tony is from Italy.
Gina *is* from Italy *and* Tony *is too.*
Bob likes to play soccer. Carlos likes to play soccer.
Bob *likes* to play soccer *and* Carlos *does too.*
Yoko can speak English. Ali can speak English.
Yoko *can* speak English *and* Ali *can too.*

E1. Combine these sentences using *and . . . too.*

1. Helen likes to go to the movies. Ann likes to go to the movies.

2. Phil is a good dancer. Betty is a good dancer.

3. Ruth can play the piano. Gary can play the piano.

Method 4a   and . . . either

Alice was not at the party last night. Bob was not at the party last night.
Alice *was not* at the party last night *and* Bob *was not either.*
Betty does not usually eat at home. Pam does not usually eat at home.
Betty *does not* usually *eat* at home *and* Pam *does not either.*
Tom cannot drive. Pat cannot drive.
Tom *cannot* drive *and* Pat *cannot either.*

E2. Combine these sentences with *and . . . either.*

1. My sister does not usually watch television very much. My brother does not usually watch television very much.

2. Sarah cannot enter college in the fall. María cannot enter college in the fall.

3. Bill was not a serious student when he was younger. Dan was not a serious student when he was younger.

Method 5a   but

Robert is not very quiet. Tom is very quiet.
Robert *is not* very quiet *but* Tom *is.*
Ann goes home every weekend. Pat does not go home every weekend.
Ann *goes* home every weekend *but* Pat *does not.*
Jean cannot sing well. Charles can sing well.
Jean *cannot* sing well *but* Charles *can.*

E3. Combine these sentences with *but.*

1. Glen can ride a horse. Jeff cannot ride a horse.
2. Frank does not wear jeans to class. Mary wears jeans to class.
3. My sister was not home last night. My brother was home last night.

**E4. Write nine sentences using Methods 3a, 4a, and 5a. Use *be* and *can* in some sentences.

WRITE

A. Think about two friends or two people in your family. How are they similar? How are they different? Write a composition comparing these two people. You may want to use some of these adjectives.

old	a little heavy	lazy	intelligent
young	slender	quiet	beautiful
tall	handsome	busy	funny
short	pretty	friendly	serious

B. Use these expressions and underline them.

1. adjective + *er than*
2. *more . . . than*
3. *some* or *any*
4. a sentence with *and . . . too*
5. a sentence with *and . . . either*
6. a sentence with *but*

C. Check your paper. Use numbers 10–17.

Next Weekend

PRACTICE

A. Review

A1. Write the correct comparison form.

1. (beautiful)   A butterfly is _____ a spider.
2. (lazy)   Bruce is _____ Alice.
3. (big)   A Buick is _____ a Toyota.
4. (tall)   Paula is _____ Carol.
5. (funny)   A monkey is _____ a lion.
6. (thin)   I am _____ my sister.
7. (delicious)   Chicken is _____ beef.

A2.   Put the correct form of a possessive pronoun in the blank.

1.   The elephant picked up the man in _____ trunk.

2.   Did you see (I) _____ book anywhere?

3.   He left _____ wallet at home by mistake.

4.   (We) _____ class is going to have a party.

5.   Next weekend Mr. and Mrs. Thomas are going to visit _____ son and daughter-in-law.

6.   Do you have _____ notebook with you today?

7.   She has to take _____ car to the garage.

8.   All of you write well. _____ compositions are very good.

A3.   Each sentence has one mistake. Find it and correct it.

WRONG

1.   I like to listen music.

2.   I sometime watch television.

3.   She is tall, she has brown hair.

4.   My brother like to play soccer.

WRONG 5.   My sister likes play tennis. **WRONG**

6.   Bob gets up at 7:00, then he takes a shower.

7.   After class I go to home.

8.   Paul usually goes to the bed at 11:30.

9.   We like to go to the movie.

10.   Pat arrives to the university at 8:30.

B.   Future (*be going to* + SV)

Use *be going to* and the simple verb for future time.

I *am going to visit* my uncle next week.
Nadia *is going to take* the TOEFL test in two weeks.
We *are going to go* to London next summer.

Negative (be + not + going to + SV)
Put *not* after *be* to form the negative.

I *am not going to visit* my uncle next week.
Nadia *is not going to take* the TOEFL test in two weeks.
We *are not going to go* to London next summer.

These are some common time expressions for the future.

tomorrow	next week	in 1990
tonight	next month	in June
tomorrow morning	next year	in three days
tomorrow afternoon	next summer	(three days from now)
tomorrow night	next vacation	in two weeks
	next Sunday	in six months
	next May	in five years

B1. **Change each sentence to the future. Use** *be going to* **and a time expression from the list.**

1. I often go to a party on Saturday night.

2. Last vacation Phil visited his grandparents.

3. Yesterday morning we had an exam.

4. Anna played tennis last Sunday.

5. They did not go to Disneyland last week.

6. Tom had a party two weeks ago.

7. Pat did not enter college in 1980.

8. Lois bought a new car last year.

9. I did not stop at the supermarket on my way home yesterday.

10. We had steak for dinner last night.

B2. **Write four sentences with *going to* **for future time. Write two affirmative and two negative sentences.**

C.   Time expressions: ago, in three days

Use *ago* for the past.

I visited Japan two years *ago*.

Six weeks *ago* he started a new English class.

Pam got a letter three days *ago*.

Use *in* for the future.

They are going to visit Japan *in* three weeks. (three weeks from now)

Tom is going to enter college *in* two months.

In five days I am going to buy a new car.

C1. Use these words to make a sentence in the past using *ago*. Then change the sentence to the future using *in*.

1. he / eat / at an expensive restaurant / two weeks
2. she / write / to her parents / two days
3. Bill / leave / for Hawaii / two months
4. they / start / college / two years
5. I / do / my homework / an hour

**C2. Write three sentences using *ago* and three using *in* as a time expression.

D. Possessives

Subject Pronoun		Possessive Adjective (with a noun)		Possessive Pronoun (without a noun)	
I	we	my	our	mine	ours
you	you	your	your	yours	yours
he		his		his	
she	they	her	their	hers	theirs
it		its		its	

Use a possessive pronoun *without* a noun.

His family lives in Caracas and *mine* lives in Tokyo.
This is my car. That is *hers*.

D1. Put the right possessive form in the blank.

1. (We) _____ team won and (they) _____ lost.
2. The red car is (she) _____ and the black one is (he) _____.
3. Does (you) _____ family live in Paris? (I) _____ lives in Montreal.
4. (He) _____ father is an engineer but (I) _____ is a doctor.
5. Are these papers (you) _____ or (we) _____?

**D2. Write four sentences using possessive pronouns.

E. Prepositions: in

Use *in* to show that something is inside something else.

My class is *in* the Modern Languages Building.
The clothes are *in* the closet.

Use *in* with geographical names and with some time expressions.

in a city (in Montreal)   in August (month)

in a state (in Kansas)   in summer (season)

in a country (in Brazil)   in 1985 (year)

in a continent (in Asia)

E1.   Put *in, at,* or *to* in the blanks.

1. My money is _____ my wallet and my wallet is _____ my pocket.

2. Mary's family lives _____ Michigan.

3. She usually carries her books _____ her backpack.

4. She is going to drive _____ the new shopping center.

5. She is going to park _____ the parking lot and walk _____ the department store.

6. Then she will meet her husband _____ the restaurant next to the department store.

7. Pierre was born _____ Quebec.

**E2.   Write three sentences using *in*.

F.   Sentence combining: because (S + V + *because* + S + V)

Because shows the reason or purpose. It answers the question "Why?" Write a subject and verb before *because* and a subject and verb after *because*. Do not begin a sentence with *because*. You will learn how to do this later.

Method 6

I have to clean my apartment. I am going to have a party.
I have to clean my apartment *because* I am going to have a party.

F1.   Combine these sentences using *because*.

1. She is going to go to Los Angeles. She wants to visit Disneyland.

2. We are going to have a picnic on Saturday. We need to relax.

3. George bought a cassette recorder. He wants to listen to English tapes.

4. Marie is studying English. She needs it for her job.

**F2.   Write four sentences using *because*.

<u>WRITE</u>

A. Write a composition about what you are going to do next weekend. Use *going to* in most of the sentences.

B. Use these expressions and underline them.

1. *because*
2. a possessive
3. *in*

C. Check your paper using numbers 10–17.

A Letter to a Friend

PRACTICE

A.   Review

A1.   Put the correct form of the verb in the blank.

1. (be)   I _____ glad that you (come) _____ here to study English next month.
2. (be)   The people here _____ very friendly.
3. (get)   I _____ a scholarship from my government. Did you?
4. (arrive)   I _____ a year ago.
5. (study)   I _____ a lot but I <u>still</u> have time to enjoy myself.

6. (spend) I __________ my last vacation in Florida.
   (visit) I __________ Disney World my first day there.
7. (sit) I __________ in the cafeteria while I
   (write) __________ this letter.

A2. Put the time word in the sentence.

1. (seldom) Life is dull at this university.
2. (always) There is something interesting happening.
3. (usually) I have five hours of classes a day.
4. (often) The college organizes a trip on Thursday afternoon.
5. (sometimes) We spend the weekend in the mountains.
6. (never) We are bored.

A3. Each sentence has a mistake. Correct it.

WRONG

1. She goes to her home at 5:00 p.m.
2. I want to study at this university business administration.
3. Olga usually spends weekend doing different things.
4. She not often is watching television.
5. She went out to dinner yesterday night.
6. They are going to go to Cairo after a week.
7. I like Tony because is a lot of fun.
8. In the afternoon I went to a movie with Alice she did not like the movie.
9. She does not have some money.
10. I visited my aunt before two months.

WRONG
WRONG

B. Modals (*will, can, may, might, should, must* + SV)

Use the simple verb after a modal. Never use *to* after a modal. Some modals have two meanings.

will = be going to
can = be able to

can = permission
may = permission

may = maybe
might = maybe

should = advice
must = have to

She *will* arrive tomorrow.
He *can* sing very well.
You *can* smoke in the hall but not in the classroom.
You *may* smoke in the hall.
I *may* go to the movies tonight but I am not sure.
I *might* go to the movies tonight but I am not sure.
You *should* study the irregular verbs. You had five of them wrong.
You *must* improve your grades or you will fail this course.

B1. Fill in the blanks with a modal.

1. I am glad you _____ be here to study English in a month.

2. You _____ bring a good bilingual dictionary with you.

3. You _____ want to stop for a few days in London but you
   _____ be here for the placement test on January 15.

4. _____ you bring me something I left at home? Ask my parents
   about it.

5. You _____ stay with me until you find an apartment.

6. You _____ want to live in a dormitory.

7. You _____ also bring something typical of our country for
   International Students Day. _____ you think of something that is
   easy to pack?

8. You _____ have a good time here but you _____ get used to
   the people and the university first.

**B2. Use *might*, *should*, and *must* in sentences.

C. Imperatives (SV with no subject)

Use the imperative form (the simple verb) to tell someone to do something. Use
it to give an order or make a request (ask someone to do something). Most of the
grammar explanations in this book use the imperative form.

There is no subject in an imperative sentence. We understand that the subject is
you but we do not write it or say it.

Please makes the sentence more polite. Use it for requests.

Please close the door.
Study the new lesson for tomorrow.
Do the exercises for homework.

C1. Change each sentence to the imperative.

1. You should bring a good bilingual dictionary with you.

2. You must get a warm winter jacket before you come.

3. Can you meet me at the airport?

4. You should be at the airport forty minutes before departure time.

5. You must have extra money for the first month.

**C2. Write four imperative sentences.

D. Possessive nouns ('s, s')

Use *'s* (apostrophe s) with the names of people or animals to show possession.

1. Add *'s* to a singular noun.
   a. *Jane's* car is in the garage.
   b. A *giraffe's* neck is very long.

2. Add only an apostrophe to a plural noun. A plural noun already has an *-s*.
   The *girl's* coat is in the closet.
   The *girls'* coats are in the closet.

3. Some irregular plural nouns do not end in *-s* . Add *'s* to both singular and plural forms.
   a. the *child's* toy
      the *children's* toys
   b. the *woman's* car
      the *women's* cars
   c. the *man's* desk
      the *men's* desk

1. a.

1. b.

2.

3.   a.

3.   b.

3. c.

D1. **Write the correct possessive form in the blank.**

1. (Ahmed) _____ composition is excellent.

2. (professor) The _____ house is near the university.

3. (monkey) A _____ tail is long and thin.

4. (cats) Our _____ names are Sam and Joe.

5. (men) The _____ room is down the hall.

6. (parents) My _____ new car is a Mercedes.

7. (teacher) You should get your _____ advice about your problem.

8. (friend) Borrow your _____ bicycle for an hour.

9. (children) This store sells _____ clothes.

10. (Anne) _____ last name is Baker.

D2. **Write four sentences using possessive nouns. Use *children* in one sentence.

E. **Prepositions: on**

on = touching something
     over and touching something

The dish is *on* the table.
The clock is *on* the wall.

on + some time expressions

on Tuesday (days)
on April 20 (dates)

also:

on television
on the radio

E1. Put *at, to, in,* or *on* in the blanks.

1. My plane leaves _____ January 9.

2. Classes start _____ Tuesday.

3. The semester finishes _____ May.

4. There is a good movie _____ television tonight.

5. I will see you _____ the airport _____ two weeks.

6. We can spend some time _____ Miami on the way _____ New York.

7. The placement test will be _____ 9:00 _____ Monday morning.

8. I listened _____ some good music _____ the radio.

9. He is going to put a map of his country _____ the kitchen wall.

10. Her daughter lives _____ Colorado but she is going to move _____ Nevada.

**E2. Write three sentences using *on.*

F. Useful expressions

do your best
be sure to + SV
first of all
on time
look forward to something (look forward to + noun)
look forward to doing something (look forward to + V-ing + noun)

F1. Fill in the blanks. Use the correct verb form. Use some expressions more than once.

1. You will do several things when you arrive. _____ you will take a placement test. You must _____ on this test.

2. You must be _____ for the placement test. Be there at 8:30.

3. You will get good grades if you always try to _____.

4. I am _____ the dance next Saturday night.

5. _____ send your application form as soon as possible.

6. I _____ seeing you here next month.

7. They look forward to (visit) _____ Niagara Falls.

**F2. Use each expression in F in a sentence.

WRITE

A. A friend is going to come here to study English. Write a letter giving that friend advice and suggestions. Give some useful and interesting information about this university or language center. (We do not usually start a letter with "How are you? I am fine." in English.)

B. Use these expressions and underline them.

1. three modals
2. two imperative sentences
3. *look forward to*
4. *be sure to*

C. Check your paper. Use numbers 10–17.

LETTER FORM

(your address)
2836 E. Speedway, Apt. 6
Tucson, Arizona 85719
December 9, 19__

Dear _____,

    I was very glad to get your letter and I am happy that you are going to come here to study English.

Your friend,
(your name)

Other closings:

Your cousin,
Your brother,
Yours truly,
Sincerely yours,

My City

PRACTICE

A. Review

A1. Use the information to write a comparison sentence using *-er* or *more . . . than.*

1. Ann is twenty years old. Laura is twenty-five.
2. Kyoto is beautiful. Osaka is not beautiful.
3. Addition is easy for children. Long division is not easy.
4. Sue is a good dancer. Mary is not a very good dancer.
5. The cost of living is high in London. The cost of living is low in a village.

A2.   Put an article (*a, an, the*) in each blank if one is necessary.

1.   My sister likes _____ sports.

2.   _____ new student entered class today.

3.   _____ new student in my class is from Spain.

4.   _____ engineer has to work hard.

5.   _____ lemons are sour.

6.   My teacher likes to help _____ people learn English.

7.   _____ food at _____ restaurant is usually better than _____ food at _____ student cafeteria.

8.   _____ population of Mexico City is around sixteen million.

A3.   Find one error in each sentence and correct it.

WRONG

1.   My parents bought some new furnitures.

2.   It was not a important.

3.   After that I study my homework.

4.   I often go to partys.

WRONG   5.   On Saturday I clean my bedroom while wash my clothes.   WRONG

6.   Yesterday I went to swimming.

7.   For lunch we ate a hamburgers.

8.   The students are eating in the cafeteria every day.

9.   I like Paris. Because it is a beautiful city.

10.   Bring winter clothes, bring summer clothes too.

B.   Comparisons (*the* + adjective + *-est, the most* + adjective, *good - best, bad - worst*)

We use adjectives to compare three or more people or things.

1.   When an adjective has one syllable, add *-est* and use *the.*
    Tom is *tall.*
    Paul is *taller than* Tom.
    Bill is *the tallest* of the three men.

2.   When an adjective has two syllables and ends in *y,* add *-est* and use *the.*
    French is *easy.*
    Spanish is *easier than* French.
    English is *the easiest* language in the world.
    Spelling: Use the *y* rule and the 1–1–1 rule before *-est.*
        busy - busier - busiest   big - bigger - biggest

3. Use *the most* with adjectives that have three or more syllables.

> Ottawa is a *beautiful* city.
> Rio de Janeiro is *more beautiful than* Ottawa.
> My city is *the most beautiful* city in the world.

4. *Good* and *bad* are irregular.

> Chocolate ice cream is *good*.
> Strawberry ice cream is *better*.
> Vanilla ice cream is *the best*.
>
> Pat is a *bad* student.
> Peter is a *worse* student *than* Pat.
> Ann is *the worst* student in the class.

SUMMARY: Comparison of Adjectives

	1 syllable*	2 syllables -y*	3 or more syllables	good	bad
Comparative (2 things)	adjective + -er than	adjective + -er than	more + adjective + than	better	worse
Superlative (3 or more things)	the + adjective + -est	the + adjective + -est	the most + adjective	best	worst

*Spelling: Use the y and the 1–1–1 rule.

B1.   **Write the two comparison forms for each adjective. Use *than* and *the*.**

1. clean
2. exciting
3. careful
4. happy
5. expensive
6. large
7. good
8. important

B2.   **Use four of the words in comparison sentences with *-est* or *the most*.

C. Many, much, a lot of

Use *many* with count nouns and *much* with noncount nouns. Use *a lot of* with both. Use *many* and *much* with questions and negatives. Use *a lot of* with all kinds of sentences.

Summary

	Count	Noncount
Affirmative	a lot of	a lot of
Negative	many a lot of	much a lot of
Questions	many a lot of	much a lot of

New York has *a lot of* high-rise buildings.
There are *not many* tall buildings in small cities.
Are there *many* modern buildings in Baghdad?
There is *a lot of* traffic during rush hours.
Is there *much* traffic on the side streets?
There is *not much* traffic at 2:00 a.m.

Here are some common noncount nouns. They do not have a plural form.

information	rain	traffic	salt
jewelry	snow	transportation	pepper
music	wind	vocabulary	fun

C1. **Write *much*, *many*, or *a lot of* in the blanks. Use *much* and *many* only where they are necessary.**

1. The main streets of Chicago have _____ traffic.
2. Are there _____ wide streets in Tokyo?
3. There are _____ parks in Ottawa.
4. There is not _____ rain in Riyadh.
5. Is there _____ homework for tomorrow?
6. You have to write _____ sentences.
7. There is not _____ new vocabulary.
8. The book does not have _____ exercises.
9. Queen Elizabeth has _____ beautiful jewelry.
10. Some students have _____ fun with their friends.

C2. **Use *many* in two sentences, *much* in two, and *a lot of* in one.

D. Prepositions: by

by = near, next to
The chair is *by* the window.

by = along, through, past
        We took a walk *by* the river.   (along or beside it)
        We entered the house *by* the side door.
        We drove *by* the new shopping center.
        (We did not stop there or go in.)

D1. Fill in the blanks with *by, at, to, in,* or *on.*

1. On your way _____ the Student Union you will walk _____ the
    Chemistry Building.

2. There are not many good programs _____ television.

3. Meet me _____ the Hilton Hotel _____ 5:00.

4. The hotel is _____ the new government buildings.

5. Enter the hotel _____ the main entrance.

6. I will wait _____ the information desk.

7. The information desk is _____ the lobby.

8. The main street goes _____ the city hall.

9. We are going on our vacation _____ June.

10. There are always a lot of people _____ the park _____ Sunday.

**D2. Write three sentences. Use *by* in three different ways.

E. Useful expressions

in a city (in New York)	high-rise buildings
on a street (on Main Street)	rush hour
at an exact address (at 1307 Main Street)	heavy traffic
the cost of living (noncount)	a traffic jam

E1. Fill in the blanks.

1. All large cities have _____ buildings.

2. There are several museums _____ Park Avenue
    _____ New York.

3. Los Angeles has a lot of freeways but during _____ the
    traffic moves slowly. Sometimes there is _____ and the
    traffic does not move at all.

4. During the rush hour in New York, there is _____ in the
    tunnels under the Hudson River.

5. The city hall is _____ 10 Government Square.

6. The _____ is higher in Washington than Atlanta.

E2.   **Use each expression in E in a sentence.

F.   **Organizing a paragraph**

> All of the sentences in this composition are good sentences, but they are not organized well. They are not in the right order. Read the paragraph and then write it again with the sentences in the right order. Combine some of the short sentences into longer ones.

MY APARTMENT

> My apartment is in Mexico City. It is small but it is beautiful. It is on the seventh floor of a large building. There are two bathrooms. There is a kitchen. There is a living room. There is a beautiful view from the balcony. There are a lot of plants in the rooms. There is a dining room. There are a lot of pictures. There are three bedrooms. It is comfortable. There are a lot of windows. I like living in this apartment.

WRITE

A.   **Describe your city in a composition.**

> You may want to use some of these words and expressions:

airport	schools	lake
factories	hotels	river
stores	beach	narrow streets
shopping center	ocean	high-rise buildings
university	mountains	traditional houses

B.   **Use these expressions and underline them.**

1. a comparison with *-est*.
2. a comparison with *the most*.
3. *much* or *many*
4. two of the expressions in E

C.   **Check your paper. Use numbers 10–18.**

Weekends

PRACTICE

A. Review

A1. Write the -s form (third person singular) of each verb.

go	finish	study
get	do	leave
wash	play	have
pass	be	copy

A2. Add the time word to the sentences.

1. (usually)   He sleeps late on Saturday morning.
2. (always)   She does her laundry on Saturday.
3. (never)   David studies on Saturday night.
4. (often)   We are very busy on Saturday.
5. (sometimes)   They go to Kennedy Park for a picnic.
6. (seldom)   Mary is home on the weekend.

A3. Write the possessive adjectives and the possessive pronouns.

Subject	Possessive Adjective (with a noun)	Possessive Pronoun (without a noun)
I		
you		
he		
she		
it		
we		
you		
they		

B.   Negative time words *(not always)*

Use *not* with *always, usually,* and *often.* Do not use it with *sometimes, seldom, rarely,* or *never.* Write (do/does) *not* before the indefinite time word.

Ruth *does not* usually get up early on Saturday.
I am *not* usually busy on Saturday.
He *never* studies on Saturday night.

B1. Change the sentences to negative if it is possible.

1. Mary usually goes shopping on Saturday night.
2. We never watch television on Saturday morning.
3. Ali is always in class on Friday afternoon.
4. Sometimes they like to go out for dinner on Saturday.
5. I often go to a disco on Friday.
6. She always eats at the student cafeteria on the weekend.
7. He is rarely home on Saturday night.
8. I usually do my homework on Friday night.

9. Susan never wants to have a picnic.

10. We are usually tired on Monday morning.

**B2. Write three sentences. Use *not always, not usually,* and *not often* in the sentences. Use *be* in one of the sentences.

C. Questions

There are two kinds of questions in English. The names come from the answers you expect.

1. Yes/no questions
   You expect *yes* or *no* as the answer.
   > Is her name Mary? Yes. (No.)
   > Do you live in a dormitory? Yes. (No.)

2. *Wh-* or information questions
   You expect some information as the answer. Most question words begin with *wh-*: who, what, where, why, when, how.
   > Her name is Mary.
   > Is her name Mary?
   > What is her name?

1. Questions with *be* (*be* + S or wh- word + *be* + S or wh- word + *be*)
   Put *be* before the subject. Put the wh- word at the beginning of the sentence.
   > A rose is a flower.
   > Is a rose a flower?
   > What is a rose?
   Do not change the word order if the wh- word is the subject.
   > *Tom* is his roommate.
   > *Who* is his roommate?

2. Questions with other verbs (*do/does* + S + SV or wh- word + *do/does* + S + SV or wh- word + V)
   Put *do/does* before the subject. Use the simple verb. The wh- question word is the first word in the sentence.
   > Tom lives in a dormitory.
   > *Does* Tom live in a dormitory?
   > *Where* does Tom live?
   > *Who* lives in a dormitory?

C1. Change each statement to a yes/no question.

1. Joe is twenty years old.
2. Tom and Sue are at a party tonight.
3. Phil works at a hospital.
4. Mr. and Mrs. Green like to play cards.
5. Don's father is an engineer.

C2. Change each sentence to a *wh-* question. Make the question about the words in *italic* type.

1. Gary is *in Syria*.

2. Carol usually eats *at the Student Union*.

3. *Tom* is Bill's roommate.

4. A pear is *a kind of fruit*.

5. Classes start *on Monday*.

6. I usually have *a sandwich* for lunch.

**C3. Write two yes/no questions and two wh- questions. Use *be* and other verbs.

D. Object pronouns

Subject Pronoun	Object Pronoun
I	me
you	you
he	him
she	her
it	it
we	us
you	you
they	them

Use object pronouns as the object of a verb or the object of a preposition.

She met *him* at a party last month.
I bought a birthday present for *her*.

D1. Fill in the blanks with object pronouns.

1. I read (that book) _____ last year.

2. He found (two baby birds) _____ in the driveway.

3. Ms. Johnson left (her daughter) _____ at the babysitter's house.

4. Ms. Johnson took (her son) _____ with (Ms. Johnson) _____.

5. My parents sent a package to (I) _____.

6. Thank (you) _____.

7. My mother woke (my brother and me) _____ up early yesterday.

**D2. Use four object pronouns in sentences. Use ones you do not know very well.

E. Useful expressions

on weekends
on the weekend
on Sundays
on Sunday

on Sunday afternoon
at a restaurant
have a party
have a picnic

E1. Fill in the blanks.

1. I often go swimming _____ weekends.

2. She usually cleans her room _____ weekend.

3. _____ Sunday we go to church.

4. Then we eat _____ restaurant.

5. He often goes out to dinner _____ Friday night.

6. I do not study very much _____ Sundays.

7. They go shopping _____ Saturday morning.

8. He usually has lunch _____ restaurant.

9. Sometimes I _____ a party at my apartment.

10. In the summer we often _____ a picnic in the mountains.

**E2. Write four sentences using some of the expressions in E.

F. Sentence combining: before, after

Put *after* with sentence A. Put *before* with sentence B. Sentence A happens first.
(*after* A, *before* B)

Method 7

       A   **B**
I have breakfast. I brush my teeth.
       A   **B**
After I have breakfast, I brush my teeth.
      B   **A**
Or: I brush my teeth after I have breakfast.

       A   **B**
I did my laundry. I went to a friend's apartment.
      A   **B**
After I did my laundry, I went to a friend's apartment.
      B   **A**
Or: I went to a friend's apartment after I did my laundry.

Method 8

            A   **B**
I made some coffee. I got dressed.

            B   **A**
Before I got dressed, I made some coffee.

            A   **B**
Or: I made some coffee before I got dressed.

            A   **B**
I wrote a letter. I went to bed.

            B   **A**
Before I went to bed, I wrote a letter.

            A   **B**
Or: I wrote a letter before I went to bed.

F1. **Combine these sentences using the word in parentheses. Put the sentences in the right order. Do each pair of sentences two ways.**

1. (after)   I get up. I take a shower.

2. (after)   They finished their homework. They went out for some pizza.

3. (before)   She makes a list. She goes shopping.

4. (before)   Pam decided to call her parents. She left for class.

F2. **Write two sentences using Method 7 and two sentences using Method 8. Write each sentence both ways. (This makes eight sentences.)

WRITE

A. Interview someone in the class. Ask what she/he usually does on the weekend. Make notes. Then write a composition about your classmate's weekends.

Ask questions like these:

What do you usually do on Saturday?
Do you go out on Saturday night?
Do you study on the weekend?

B. Use these expressions and underline them.

1. *not* with *usually* or *often*
2. an object pronoun
3. a prepositional phrase at the beginning of a sentence
4. connecting words like *then* or *and then*
5. combine two sentences with *before* or *after*

C. Check your paper. Use numbers 10–18.

A Vacation

PRACTICE

A. Review

A1. Write the past tense of each verb.

read	meet	begin
feel	send	sleep
make	do	leave
drive	buy	find
cost	teach	lend
spend	take	be
wake		write

A2. **Write each sentence in the past tense. Then write it in the negative past tense. Change the time expressions.**

1. Carol spends her vacation at the beach every year.

2. Mary goes to Hawaii every winter.

3. They often visit museums and famous buildings on their vacation.

4. We go swimming every day.

5. They go camping in the mountains every summer.

A3. **Each sentence has one mistake. Correct it.**

WRONG

1. It was wonderful weekend.

2. On Sunday I called with my parents.

3. I back home.

4. I went to the cafeteria and had lunch in it.

WRONG 5. I ate dinner after I went to bed. WRONG

6. Saturday in the morning I got up at 10:00.

7. I got up at 11:00. ^and̾ And then I had breakfast.

8. I got up early. After I had breakfast.

9. The weather very nice every day.

10. I visited they for two weeks.

B. **Past tense questions**

1. *Be (was/were + S or wh- words + was/were + S or wh- words + be)*
   Past tense questions are like present tense questions, but we use the past tense of *be (was/were)*.

   > She was at the beach yesterday.
   > *Was she* at the beach yesterday?
   > *Where was she* yesterday?
   > *Who was* at the beach yesterday?

2. Other verbs (*did* + S + SV or wh- word + *did* + S + SV or wh- word + V)
   Past tense questions with other verbs are like present tense questions but we use the past tense of *do (did)*. Use the simple form of the other verb.

   > He went to Japan last summer.
   > *Did he go* to Japan last summer?
   > *Where did he go* last summer?
   > *Who went* to Japan last summer?

B1. **Change each sentence to a yes/no question in the past tense.**

1. John spent last summer in Canada.

2. He was in Quebec.

3. Pat went to South America for her summer vacation.

4. Sue enjoyed her vacation in Europe.

5. Don's brothers were in Tokyo for a month.

B2.   **Change each sentence to a wh- question in the past tense.**

1. They went to California.

2. Paul stayed at a hotel.

3. He arrived late at night.

4. She visited her aunt and uncle.

5. Ms. Brown bought a beautiful handmade sweater.

6. Tom was in China.

B3.   **Write two yes/no questions and two wh- questions. Use *be* and other verbs in the past tense.

C.   Irregular verbs

Learn these verb forms:

choose–chose	forget–forgot	see–saw	lose–lost
speak–spoke	bring–brought	put–put	ride–rode
drink–drank	think–thought	wea'–wore	lie–lay

C1.   **Write the past tense of the correct verb in the blank.**

1. We _____ on the beach in the afternoon.

2. I _____ my shorts and bathing suits most of the time.

3. I _____ Disneyland and Sea World.

4. Phil _____ his suitcases in the car.

5. He _____ his watch at the beach. He never found it.

6. We never _____ about our jobs during our vacation.

7. She _____ some souvenirs home with her.

8. They _____ on a bus for six hours.

9. We _____ a lot of soft drinks because the weather was hot.

10. Marie _____ English for three hours yesterday.

11. I _____ a bright-colored shirt as a souvenir of Hawaii.

12. I _____ to write any post cards.

C2.   **Use the past tense of five of the verbs in sentences. Choose verbs you do not know very well.

D.   Count and noncount nouns

1.   Use a plural noun with these expressions:

several   There are *several* large *buildings* on my campus.
one of   *One of* the *buildings* is new.
different   My classes are in *different buildings.*
numbers   There are *three* cafeterias in the Student Union.

2.   Use a plural noun and a plural verb form

OR

use a noncount noun and a singular verb form after these expressions:

a lot of   There are *a lot of chairs* in my classroom.
There is *a lot of furniture* in my house.
most of   *Most of* my *classes* are in the same building.
Most of the *furniture* in the classroom is new.
some of   *Some of* the *chairs* are green.
Some of the *chalk* is yellow.

D1.   Write the correct form of the noun.

1.   New York has several (university) _____.

2.   Most of the (building) _____ at my university are large.

3.   There are a lot of foreign (student) _____ at UCLA.

4.   Students from different (country) _____ speak different

(language) _____.

5.   Six (student) _____ in my class are from Malaysia.

6.   I spent most of my (money) _____.

7.   One of my (friend) _____ is from Canada.

8.   Some of the (bread) _____ is hard.

9.   We drank a lot of orange (juice) _____.

10.   Some of the (orange) _____ are not sweet.

**D2.   Use four of the expressions in *D* in sentences.

E.   Prepositions: from ... to

Use *from ... to* for time and places.

We were in Canada *from* July 1 *to* August 15.
We drove *from* Barcelona *to* Madrid.

**E1.   Write two sentences using *from ... to*. Write one about time and one about places.

F. Useful expressions

visit a place
go to a place
on (my) vacation
spend my vacation

late at night
stay up
spend time/a day/three weeks/two years
to get to someplace (arrive)

F1. Fill in the blanks. Use some expressions more than once.

1. We _____ Disney World too late to see anything that night.

2. Last summer I _____ Greece for the first time.

3. Peter usually _____ his vacation at the beach.

4. The Holts are planning to go to Bermuda _____ their vacation.

5. Mr. Hayes is not at work. He is _____ vacation.

6. _____ her last vacation she visited her family.

7. We stayed until late _____.

8. We _____ two weeks in Rome and had a very good time.

9. They _____ a long time at the airport because the plane was late.

**F2. Use five of the expressions in F in sentences. Choose ones you do not know very well.

WRITE

A. Think about all of your vacations. Choose one that was very special in some way and write about it.

B. Use these expressions and underline them.

1. a negative sentence
2. three irregular verbs
3. one of the expressions in D
4. two of the expressions in F

C. Check your paper using numbers 10–18.

Another Letter

PRACTICE

A. Review

A1. Add *-ing* to each verb.

stay	lie	make
put	write	study
travel	fly	get
marry	stop	drive

A2. Change each sentence to the present continuous. Change each time expression to *now*.

1. I stayed at a beautiful hotel last year.
2. We write sentences every day.

3. Ms. Frank visits her daughter every year.

4. They usually have dinner at 6:30.

5. Carl often plays tennis on Saturday.

A3. **Combine these sentences with *and . . . too, and . . . either,* or *but.***

1. Dan likes to play baseball. Ali does not like to play baseball.

2. Lois has lunch at the Student Union every day. Bob has lunch at the Student Union every day.

3. Gary does not usually spend Saturday at his apartment. Tony does not usually spend Saturday at his apartment.

4. Keiko is from Japan. Yoko is from Japan.

5. John cannot come to our party. Carol can come to our party.

B. Present continuous: questions and negatives

1. Questions (*be* + S + V-ing, wh- word + *be* +S + V-ing)
   Put *be* before the subject to form a question. The *wh-* word is the first word in the sentence.

   > The teacher *is explaining* the lesson.
   > Is the teacher explaining the lesson?
   > What is the teacher explaining?

2. Negatives (S + *be* + *not* + V-ing)
   Put *not* after *be* to form the negative.

   > My brother *is not* studying in New York this year.

B1. **Change each sentence to a present continuous yes/no question. Then change it to a wh- question. Change the time expression to *now.***

1. Did you study Chinese last year?

2. Your little sister is playing at her friend's house.

3. The Morgans watched a good television program last night.

4. Ann usually stays at the Holiday Inn.

B2. **Change each sentence to the negative present continuous.**

1. The students are taking an exam now.

2. Paul is working in Europe this year.

3. Ms. Fiori is visiting her sister this week.

4. Tony is sitting by the window.

**B3. Write two yes/no questions, two wh- questions, and two negative sentences in the present continuous tense.

C. *Very* and *too* (*too* + adjective + *to* + V = *too young to drive*)

Very makes an adjective stronger.

The weather was hot.
The weather was *very* hot.
We live in an old house.
We live in a *very* old house.

Too means *too much*. It gives the sentence a negative feeling or idea. We often write *to* and a simple verb after a *too* phrase.

The weather was *too cold to go swimming*.
(We could not go swimming.)
Our daughter is *too young to drive*.
(She cannot drive.)
Ann was *too tired to go out* in the evening.
(She did not go out.)

C1. Put *very* or *too* in each blank.

1. That used car is _____ cheap, but it is a good car for the price.
2. That used car is _____ old to buy. I do not want to spend a lot of money on repairs.
3. This red shirt is _____ bright, but I like it.
4. That red shirt is _____ bright. I do not like it.
5. These jeans are _____ expensive for him to buy.
6. These jeans are _____ expensive, but he is going to buy them anyway.
7. Our English lesson was _____ long for me to do in an hour.
8. Our English lesson was _____ long but I was able to do it in an hour.
9. My coffee is _____ hot for me to drink right now.
10. I am not _____ hungry. I ate _____ much ice cream this afternoon.

**C2. Write two sentences with *very* and two with *too*.

D. Travel expressions

Use *by* for ways to travel if there is only one word after *by*.

by plane	*by* ship
by car	*by* bicycle
by bus	

They went to Amsterdam *by* plane.
We are going to Montreal *by* bus.

Other travel expressions:

They are going to fly to Amsterdam.
They took the bus downtown.
I come to class on the bus.
Ann comes to class on her bicycle.
He walks to class.
I usually come to class with my brother in his car.

D1.   **Use four of the travel expressions in sentences.

E. Useful expressions

wait for	to board a plane
buy something for someone	a plane lands
do something for someone	a plane takes off
write a letter to someone	

E1.   **Fill in the blanks.**

1.   I am waiting _____ my plane.

2.   I am writing a letter _____ you.

3.   My husband is buying a present _____ our daughter.

4.   Some people are _____ a plane for New York.

5.   One plane is _____ off and another one _____ two minutes ago.

6.   A man is getting some coffee _____ his wife.

7.   A porter is carrying some luggage _____ a passenger.

E2.   **Use five of the expressions in E in sentences.

F.   **Combining sentences:** *and . . . too, and . . . either, but* **with present continuous**

Method 3b

Ali is studying English.
Albert is studying English.
Ali *is* studying English *and* Albert *is too.*

Method 4b

Helen is not living in a dormitory this year.
Betty is not living in a dormitory this year.
Helen *is not* living in a dormitory this year *and* Betty *is not either.*

Method 5b

The new students are taking a placement test now.
The continuing students are not taking a placement test now.
The new students *are* taking a placement test now *but* the continuing students *are not.*

F1.   **Combine these sentences.**

1.   The baby is sleeping. The other children are not sleeping.

2.   Marie is helping her mother. Jean is helping her mother.

3.   I am not wearing jeans today. Paul is not wearing jeans today.

F2.   **Write three sentences. Write one using Method 3b, one using 4b, and one using 5b.

<u>WRITE</u>

A. You are sitting in the airport waiting for your plane. You have enough time to write a letter to a friend. Tell the friend what you are doing. What are other people doing? Where are you going? Write a letter using the present continuous in most of the sentences. Use the letter form on page 66.

B. Use these expressions and underline them.

1. a negative present continuous sentence
2. *very*
3. *too*

C. Check your paper using numbers 10–18.

1. Usually/Everyday/Teacher/Wear   Today

2. Usually/Everyday/Student   Today

3. Usually/Everyday/Doctor   Today

Usually/Today

4. Usually/Everyday/Architect

Today

PRACTICE

A. Review

A1. Write the plural form of each count noun. Do not write anything for the noncount nouns.

question	clothes	peach
information	rain	traffic
homework	song	meat
skirt	wife	baby
salt	child	music
	fruit	

A2. **This paragraph is not organized well. Write it again with the sentences in the right order. Combine some short sentences to make longer sentences.**

MY HOUSE

I live in a large house. It is white. There is a garage. It has a living room and a dining room. There are three bedrooms. There are trees and flowers in the yard. In my bedroom I have a stereo and a television. There is a kitchen. The furniture is very nice. I like living in this house with my family.

A3. **Find one mistake in each sentence and correct it.**

WRONG

1. There are seven childrens in my family.

2. She leaves at the university at 4:30.

3. He arrive home late in the afternoon.

4. She goes to bed early in the night.

5. He arrives at university at 8:00 a.m.

6. She has a dinner at 6:30.

7. She is a teacher very nice.

8. I am going to Peru for my vacations.

9. I am going there after one month.

10. I am going in a plane.

B. **Present continuous and present**

Most verbs describe an action.

write	run	grow	go
study	walk	watch	spend
listen	think		

Some verbs describe a condition or situation. We do not usually use these verbs in the present continuous.

be	see	hear	like
want	know	mean	understand
need	have (possess)		

I *am watching* television now.
I *see* some people outside the building.
She *is listening* to some soft music.
She *hears* a bird singing.
He *wants* his pen back right now.
I *have* a new car.
She *needs* some more paper.
They *understand* the question and they *know* the answer.

B1. **Put the correct verb form in the blank.**

1. (fight) Stop those children! They _____.

2. (understand) I _____ what you are saying.

3. (need) The doctor _____ another nurse in the office.

4. (watch) I am sitting here in the park and _____ the people.

5. (see) I _____ children and adults.

6. (walk) They _____ near the lake.

7. (have) Some of them _____ dogs with them.

8. (hear) I _____ a strange noise!

9. (want) David _____ a new car.

10. (have) He _____ a bicycle now.

11. (listen) I _____ to music and doing my homework.

B2. **Use these words in sentences about the present: *see, watch, hear, listen, need, write.*

C. **Like to/would like to (would like to = want to)**

Would like to means *want to.* Use it for the future.

I *would like to* visit Hawaii.
(I want to visit Hawaii.)
Would you *like to* go to the basketball game tonight?
(Do you want to go to the basketball game tonight?)

Like to tells an opinion or information.

She *likes to* watch television.
He *liked to* play soccer when he was a child.

C1. **Put *would like to* or *like to* in each blank.**

1. They _____ listen to music when they are too tired to study.

2. _____ you _____ hear my new cassette?

3. She _____ study business administration next year.

4. I do not _____ watch football games.

5. When Ruth was younger she _____ go to a disco.

6. I _____ speak English perfectly but I cannot.

7. Paul usually _____ do his homework in the evening.

8. Tomorrow he _____ go out to dinner.

**C2.   Write two sentences with *like to* and two with *would like to*.

D.   Verb + *to* + simple verb

Some verbs have *to* after them if the next word is a verb. Always use the simple form of the second verb.

want to	try to	plan to	expect to
begin to	decide to	like to	have to (must)
learn to			

I *want to go* to the basketball game tonight.
He *tried to call* you last night but the line was busy.
She *has to study* for a test tomorrow. (She must study.)
I usually go right home after class but today I *decided to go* shopping.
He *is planning to visit* my family next month.
She *learned to dance* when she was in high school.

**D1.   Write five sentences using verbs in D. Choose verbs you do not know very well.

E.   Wear / put on / get dressed / a dress

In the morning Bill *gets dressed*. He *puts on* his underwear, a shirt, pants, socks, and shoes. He *wears* these clothes all day. At 11:00 p.m. he *puts on* his pajamas and goes to bed. Sometimes he *wears* shorts in summer. In the winter he *wears* a jacket. He never wears *a dress*. Women wear *dresses*.

E1.   Fill in the blanks.

1. Sometimes on Saturday morning I do not _____ until noon.

2. If I feel cold I _____ a sweater.

3. When Mary _____ this morning, she _____ a dress.

4. Do young people in your country _____ jeans?

5. The weather is cold. You should _____ a jacket before you go out.

6. Who is _____ something green today?

7. Babies cannot _____ by themselves.

**E2.   Use *wear, put on, get dressed*, and *a dress* in sentences.

WRITE

A. Write one or two sentences for each pair of pictures at the beginning of the lesson. Write about what the person usually does and what he/she is doing today. Use the present and the present continuous. Make the sentences interesting.

B. Use the present and present continuous to write about five situations. Write about anything you want to.

C. Check your paper. Use numbers 10, 13, and 17.

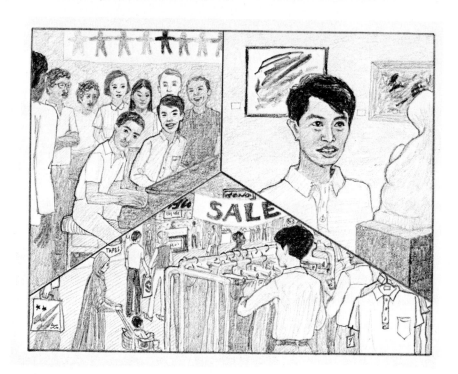

Since My Arrival

PRACTICE

A. Review

A1. Write the past tense of each verb.

carry	forget	spend
stop	see	go
walk	happen	clap
lose	meet	have
ride	speak	buy
	get	

A2. Write *some* or *any* in the blanks.

1. I saw _____ foreign films last year.

2. He did not visit _____ museums.

3. She never buys _____ clothes at the supermarket.

4. Do you have _____ novels I can borrow?

5. Ms. Peterson bought her children _____ new clothes.

6. Do you want _____ more coffee?

7. We did not get _____ mail today.

A3. Each sentence has one mistake. Correct it.

WRONG

1. David wears his clothes after he takes a shower.

2. The Johnsons drove from Paris and Rome.

3. She speaks English too well.

4. Mary usually is at home in the afternoon.

5. I can go to the party but I do not want.

6. I like to stay up late in the night.

7. We spent a good time in the mountains.

8. Last night we ate in a new restaurant.

9. I plan to visiting my parents next weekend.

10. She was born on June.

B. Past participles

There are two kinds of participles. The present participle is the *-ing* form of the verb—for example, *going* and *talking*.

1. The past participle of regular verbs is the same as the past form. Add *-ed* to the simple verb.

Simple Form	Past	Past Participle
talk	talked	talked
listen	listened	listened

2. You must memorize the past participle of irregular verbs.

Simple Form	Past	Past Participle
eat	ate	eaten
take	took	taken
get	got	gotten
buy	bought	bought
do	did	done
speak	spoke	spoken
see	saw	seen

Simple Form	Past	Past Participle
meet	met	met
go	went	gone
make	made	made
be	was/were	been
teach	taught	taught

C. Present perfect tense

The present perfect tense shows that an action or condition started in the past, is continuing now, and will probably continue into the future. When the person thinks about this action or condition, she/he connects the past action to the present time. He/she sees a connection between the past and the present. Maybe the person will continue or repeat the action or condition.

Mary *has been* here for two months. (She came in January. Now it is March and she is still here. She will probably be here for several months.)

Since I arrived I *have gone* to two shopping centers, an interesting museum, and a large park. (I will be here for two years and I will probably visit many more places.)

Tony *has taken* twenty pictures this week. (Today is Thursday. Tony started taking pictures on Monday. The week is not finished and he might take some more pictures.)

C1.   Put the correct past participle in the blanks.

1. (see)   I have _____ three movies this month.

2. (eat)   Ann has _____ lunch in the Student Union every day this week.

3. (be)   Ali has _____ to two classes since 8:00 a.m.

4. (buy)   Dan has _____ three new shirts since May.

5. (be)   Marie has _____ here a week and she has

   (make)   _____ friends with some of the students in her class.

6. (go)   She has _____ to three parties since she arrived.

7. (meet)   Paulo has _____ some other students from Brazil this month.

8. (got)   He has _____ good grades on all his quizzes.

9. (take)   We have _____ a lot of pictures since Sunday.

10. (do)   We have _____ a lot of different things since we arrived.

11. (teach)   The reading teacher has _____ us a lot of new words this week.

12. (speak)   I have _____ a lot of English since my first day here.

D. For/since

We often use *for* and *since* with the present perfect. Use *for* with a period of time. Use *since* for a point in time such as a day, date, month, or year.

Ali has been here *for* six months.
He has been here *since* January.
He has studied English *since* he was a child.

D1.   Put *for* or *since* in each blank.

1. I have owned this car _____ two years.

2. She has visited six different cities _____ she arrived.

3. He has liked sports _____ he was a child.

4. Pam has wanted to see the Grand Canyon _____ she saw a movie about it.

5. Keiko has collected stamps _____ ten years.

6. John has been able to play the piano _____ he was small.

7. Jeff has waited for this letter _____ four days.

8. They have lived in Wisconsin _____ six years.

9. I have bought a lot of clothes _____ I got here.

10. My doctor has practiced medicine _____ eight years.

D2.   Write a present perfect sentence for each situation. Use the verb in the second sentence of each pair.

1. I liked to play soccer when I was a child. I like to play it now.

2. I started taking a lot of pictures when I arrived. I am taking pictures this week.

3. Gary moved to Quebec ten years ago. He lives in Quebec now.

4. Phil arrived here in August. He is here now.

5. Ruth arrived three years ago. She is still here.

6. Yoko started studying English four years ago. She is studying it now.

D3.   Write the correct verb form in the blank.

1. (go)   I _____ to New Orleans last month.

2. (live)   He _____ in Paris for a year but he is going to move.

3. (study)   I _____ English now.

4. (study)   I _____ English for six months.

5. (study)   Ali _____ English in 1980 and then he stopped.

6. (make)   Keiko _____ friends with several Europeans since she arrived.

7. (see)   I _____ several movies on television last week.

8. (watch)   I _____ three excellent programs this week.

9. (take)   We _____ three trips since September.

10. (be)   Tom _____ to two football games this month.

**D4.   Write four sentences using the present perfect. Use *for* or *since* in each sentence.

E.   Useful expressions

have been to to tour	go on a tour arrive *in* a city (arrive in Chicago)	take a trip go sightseeing

E1.   Fill in the blanks.

1. We _____ sightseeing every day when we were in New York.

2. I am going to go _____ _____ tour of a large automobile factory.

3. Jeff has _____ to Japan and Hong Kong.

4. The Browns _____ _____ every summer.

5. Next year they are going to _____ Australia.

6. We arrived _____ Paris on Sunday.

WRITE

A.   Write a composition about what you have done since you arrived here. Tell about some interesting things but also tell about something funny or unpleasant that happened. Tell about several things you have done. Do not write in detail about just one thing. Use the present perfect for most of the sentences.

B.   Use these expressions and underline them.

1. *for*
2. *since*
3. three irregular past participles
4. *some* or *any*

C.   Check your paper using numbers 10, 13, 17, and 18.

A Biography

PRACTICE

A. Review

A1. Write the correct form of the verb in the blank.

1. Marie (born) _____ in Montreal, Quebec.

2. Tom (study) _____ at Harvard University next year.

3. Yoko (study) _____ English since she was in high school.

4. Carlos (be) _____ from Lima, Peru.

5. When she (be) _____ a child, she (like)

    _____ to (play) _____ with her cousins.

6. Carlos (like) _____ sports since he (be)

    _____ a child.

7. Keiko (study) _____ English now. She (plan)

_____ to (study) _____ business

administration after her English course.

A2. Write the past and past participle of these verbs.

take	eat
buy	go
be	do
make	get
see	meet
teach	speak

A3. Combine these sentences with *after* or *before*.

1. (after) I finished primary school. I started secondary school.
2. (before) I had to take an entrance exam. I could enter college.
3. (before) He visited all his relatives. He left for the United States.
4. (after) She moved to San Francisco. She made a lot of new friends.

B. Irregular verbs

Learn these verb forms.

Simple Form	Past	Past Participle
leave	left	left
grow	grew	grown
lose	lost	lost
write	wrote	written
sleep	slept	slept
feel	felt	felt
come	came	come
send	sent	sent
spend	spent	spent
drive	drove	driven
ride	rode	ridden
forget	forgot	forgotten

B1. Fill in the blanks with the past or present perfect.

1. (drive) She _____ 500 miles this month.
2. (sleep) I _____ eight hours last night.

3. (be)   He _____ born in Bolivia but he

    (grow)   _____ up in Peru.

4. (send)   I _____ my application to the university last

    month.

5. (write)   Marie _____ several excellent compositions this

    semester.

6. (spent)   George _____ a lot of time in the games room

    this semester.

7. (lose)   Tom _____ a lot of money in Las Vegas.

8. (come)   Phil _____ to class every day this semester.

9. (forget)   I cannot remember your name. I _____ it.

10. (leave)   Liz _____ for home yesterday.

11. (feel)   She _____ sick all this week.

12. (ride)   Larry _____ his bicycle to the university this

    morning.

**B2.   Use two of the verbs in past tense sentences and two in present perfect
         sentences.

C.   Used to (*used to* + SV)

We often use *used to* to show habitual action in the past. Use the simple verb
after *used to*.

When I was a child, I *used to* play with my friends every day.
Pat *used to* study hard when she was in high school.

C1.   Change each sentence to a sentence with *used to*.

1. She went to the beach every summer when she was small.

2. He drove to his parents' house every weekend when he was in college.

3. Jean spent the summer at her grandparents'.

4. Frank played on the basketball team.

5. When we lived in New York we went to the theater a lot.

**C2.   Write three sentences with *used to* to show habitual past action.

D.   Prepositions: *by* + V-ing

By + V-ing tells how to do something. It answers the question, "How?"

David learned to play the guitar *by practicing* every day.
(How did David learn to play the guitar?)
Pierre found out the answer *by asking* a classmate.
(How did Pierre find out the answer?)

A preposition must have a noun after it. The noun form of a verb is the V-ing form. When we use V-ing as a noun, we call it a *gerund*. (*To* is different. *To* usually has the simple verb after it.)

D1.   Answer these questions using *by* + V-ing. Write complete sentences.

1.   How did Ali improve his compositions?

2.   How can you find the post office?

3.   How can you welcome a new student?

4.   How can you improve your listening comprehension?

5.   How did Tom earn $1,000?

**D2.   Write three sentences using *by* + V-ing.

E.   Useful expressions

on May 6 (date)	start school or college	attend school
in May (month)	enter school or college	go to school
in 1970 (year)	take a test or exam	grow up
make friends	pass a test or exam	get married

E1.   Fill in the blanks.

1.   Mary was born _____, 1965.

2.   Her birthday is _____ August.

3.   It is _____ August 12.

4.   Tony _____ the TOEFL test last month but he did not

_____ it.

5.   Peter was born in Alberta but he _____ up in Ottawa.

6.   Bill can _____ college when he finishes secondary school.

7.   He is going to _____ married when he finishes college.

8.   Susan _____ school when she _____ six years old.

9. She _____ primary school in Quebec. Then she _____ secondary school in Toronto.

10. Sometimes it is hard to _____ friends at a new school.

E2. Use four of the expressions in E in a sentence. Use the ones you do not know very well.

F. Sentence combining: when

Method 9

Mary was six. She started school.
When Mary was six she started school.
OR: Mary started school *when* she was six.

F1. Combine these pairs of sentences using *when*. Do each one two ways. Write the person's name in the first part of the sentence.

1. Peter was eighteen. He entered college.
2. Ann's family moved to Vancouver. She was twelve.
3. Ali liked to play soccer. He was a little boy.
4. Sarah was in secondary school. She decided to study English.

F2. Write three sentences using Method 9. Do each one two ways.

WRITE

A. Interview someone in the class. Use this list to ask questions and make notes. Then write a biography of the student.

Paragraph 1

1. What is your name?
2. Where and when were you born?
3. What kind of work do your parents do?
4. How many people are there in your family?

Paragraph 2

1. Where did you go to primary and secondary school?
2. What are some interesting things that happened to you when you were a child?
3. What did you like to do in your free time when you were a child?

Paragraph 3

1. Did you come here to study English right after you finished secondary school?
2. Why do you want to learn English?
3. Why did you decide to study here?
4. What do you plan to do when you finish this English course?

Paragraph 4

1. Are you married or single?
2. What do you like to do in your free time?

Paragraph 5

1. Think about everything the person told you. Write a good concluding paragraph.

B. Use these expressions and underline them.

1. two sentences combined with *when*
2. two sentences combined with *before* or *after*
3. four irregular verbs
4. a sentence with *used to*

C. Check your paper. Use numbers 10, 13, 17, and 18.

A Childhood Experience

PRACTICE

A. Review

A1. Write the past tense of these verbs.

drink	bring	leave
feel	put	come
wear	send	drive
choose	cost	find
lie	grow	wake
think	teach	lend
lose	speak	

A2. Write the correct words in the chart.

Subject Pronoun	Object Pronoun	Possessive Adjective	Possessive Pronoun
I			
you			
he			
she			
it			
we			
you			
they			

A3. Make a question or a negative sentence in the present continuous tense using these words. Add any necessary words.

1. where / you / go
2. not / he / listen / teacher
3. Mary / work / in / office
4. what / you / think / about
5. not / Mark / feel / well / today

B. Irregular verbs

Learn these verb forms.

Simple Form	Past	Past Participle
fight	fought	fought
understand	understood	understood
tell	told	told
hide	hid	hidden
wear	wore	worn
know	knew	known
hurt	hurt	hurt
let	let	let
ring	rang	rung
sing	sang	sung
drink	drank	drunk
win	won	won

B1. Fill in the blanks with the correct verb form.

1. Mother _____ me go to the park alone.
2. My father _____ me to stay away from the car.

3. I _____ her all my life.

4. He used to _____ with his brother all the time.

5. Mother _____ to me to put me to sleep when I was little.

6. Did you _____ the question?

7. _____ you ever _____ Japanese tea?

8. She _____ her leg in an accident.

9. I used to like to _____ jeans all the time.

10. The phone _____ at 2:00 last night.

11. My brother _____ behind the wall and frightened me.

12. Our soccer team _____ most of the games.

B2.   **Use four of these verbs in past tense sentences.

C.   Past continuous (*was/were* + V-ing)

The past continuous is like the present continuous. Use *was/were* instead of *am/is/are*. Use this tense for a continuous action in the past. We often use the past continuous to show that one action interrupted another. Use the simple past for the action that interrupted something.

I *was eating* dinner when the phone *rang*.
They *were talking* to each other when I *interrupted* them.

C1.   **Write the correct verb forms in the blanks.**

1. I (read) _____ when my father (call) _____ me.

2. We (drive) _____ down the street when a car (pull) _____ out in front of us.

3. Sue (write) _____ a letter when Mary (arrive) _____.

4. They (have) _____ lunch at the Student Union when they (see) _____ an old friend walk by.

5. The students (talk) _____ when the teacher (enter) _____ the classroom.

C2.   **Write three sentences using the past continuous and simple past.

D.   Could = was able to (S + *could* + SV)

Can shows the ability to do something. *Could* is the past tense of *can*. Use the simple verb form without *to* after *can* or *could*.

Tom *can* run ten kilometers.
He *could* run five kilometers last year.

Put *not* after *can* or *could* to form the negative. *Cannot* is one word and *could not* is two words. (*Could* has other meanings too. You will learn them later.)

George *cannot* run ten kilometers.
He *could not* run ten kilometers last year either.

D1. Write *can* or *could* in each blank.

1. I was late for class because I _____ not start my car this morning.

2. They _____ meet us at 6:00 tonight.

3. He wanted to do his homework but he _____ not because he had to study for a quiz.

4. Ann expected to meet Alice at the shopping center but she _____ not find her.

5. I invited them to my party tomorrow but they _____ not come.

E. Useful expressions

each other	by 6:00 (at 6:00 or before 6:00 but
think about	not after 6:00)
on the way	by this afternoon / Tuesday / next week /
get ready (prepare)	June 30

E1. Fill in the blanks. Use some expressions more than once.

1. I have to _____ for my trip. I have to buy a few things and pack my suitcases.

2. The students were talking excitedly to _____.

3. You must be there _____ 1:00. You can come earlier than that but you must not be late.

4. _____ to class this morning I saw an accident.

5. If you are not at the airport _____ 7:30 you will be too late to check in.

6. I was _____ studying electrical engineering but I decided to study electronics instead.

7. Can you have the papers ready _____ next Wednesday? I must have them then.

8. I am not sure that I want to go to Toronto but I will think _____ it.

**E2. Use five of the expressions in sentences.

F. Sentence combining: while (S + V + *while* + S + V) (*when* + past, *while* + past continuous)

> **Method 10**
>
> We often use *while* or *when* to combine a past tense sentence and a past continuous tense sentence. *While* is always with the past continuous part of the sentence. *When* is always with the past tense part of the sentence. This kind of sentence shows that one action interrupted another action.
>
> The phone rang *while* I *was eating* dinner.
> I was eating dinner *when* the phone *rang*.
> I interrupted him *while* he *was studying*.
> He was studying *when* I *interrupted* him.

> **F1.** Combine these pairs of sentences using *while*. Then combine them using *when*. Use the person's name in the first part of the sentence.
>
> 1. Dan was standing in line. A friend walked by.
> 2. She was getting dinner. Someone knocked at the door.
> 3. We were leaving the house. The telephone rang.
> 4. Charles was reading quietly. He heard a loud crash.

**F2. Write two sentences using *while* with the past continuous and past tense.

WRITE

A. Think about something that happened to you when you were a child. It might be something pleasant, unpleasant, funny, or wonderful. Write a composition about it.

B. Use these expressions and underline them.

> 1. the past continuous in two sentences
> 2. two irregular verbs from any lesson
> 3. an expression from E
> 4. two sentences combined with *while*

C. Check your paper using numbers 10, 14, 17, and 18.

Another Interview

PRACTICE

A. Review

A1. Write the correct possessive form of the nouns in parentheses.

1. The (children) _____ toys are all over the floor.
2. (Nadia) _____ parents live in Bahrain.
3. My (dentist) _____ office is near the university.
4. The (girls) _____ bicycles are against the wall.
5. Her (family) _____ summer house is on a lake.
6. The (men) _____ clothing department is on the second floor.
7. Our pet (turtle) _____ food is all gone.

A2. **Change each sentence to the present perfect. Add an appropriate time expression.**

1. Paul works for a large company.
2. Dan is a mechanical engineer.
3. Carol spent a lot of money last week.
4. Jean is studying English.
5. Mr. Howard visited several countries in South America last year.

A3. **Write the past and past participle of each verb.**

understand	hurt
drive	let
grow	come
fight	tell
leave	spend
know	write
sleep	feel
ride	lose
forget	win
hide	wear

B. Irregular verbs

Learn these verb forms.

Simple Form	Past	Past Participle
think	thought	thought
find	found	found
read	read	read
build	built	built
mean	meant	meant
stand	stood	stood
keep	kept	kept
begin	began	begun
have	had	had
catch	caught	caught
sell	sold	sold
break	broke	broken

B1. **Write the correct form of a verb in the blanks.**

1. Have you _____ a new apartment yet?
2. We have _____ Lesson 21.

3. My parents _____ a new house last year.

4. What did you _____ of that television show last night?

5. Have you _____ your old car yet?

6. We have _____ a lot of homework this week.

7. Ruth _____ by the door when she first entered the classroom.

8. I have _____ three books this month.

9. Abdulrahman _____ his new watch yesterday.

10. Phil used to _____ all his papers in his textbook.

11. She _____ to say "soup" but she said "soap."

12. Did you _____ a cold?

**B2.   Use four of the verbs in past or present perfect sentences.

C. Present perfect questions (*have/has* + S + past participle, wh- word + *have/has* + S + past participle)

Put the subject between *have/has* and the past participle to make a yes/no question in the present perfect. The wh- word is the first word in the sentence.

> She has been at the Student Union all morning.
> Has she been at the Student Union all morning?

Where has she been all morning?

We often use *ever* in a present perfect question. The question means the same without *ever*.

Have you *ever* been to London?
Have you *ever* taken a biology course?
Have you *ever* eaten Indian food?
Have you *ever* flown in a small plane?

C1.   Change these statements to yes/no questions.

1. She has left for home.

2. They have lived here for four months.

3. He has read the assignment.

4. Keiko has done her homework.

C2.   Change these statements to *wh-* questions about the words in *italic* type.

1. Tom has spoken English to *the new students and his roommate* today.

2. Ruth has stayed home all week *because she was sick.*

3. Jeff has lived *in Mexico* since he finished college.

4. They have gone to the supermarket *because they need food for their party.*

**C3. Write two yes/no questions and two wh- questions in the present perfect.

D. Questions with *how* + adjective

how much	how long	how old
how many	how far	how big

I have twenty dollars with me.
How much money do you have with you?
I have two brothers and a sister.
How many brothers and sisters do you have?
It is fifteen blocks to the immigration office.
How far is it to the immigration office?
I am twenty-one years old.
How old are you?
Mexico City has a population of 16 million.
How big is Mexico City?
Tom has lived here for three years.
How long has Tom lived here?

D1. Change each statement to a question using *how* + adjective.

1. She has been here for two years.
2. He is twenty.
3. The semester is fourteen weeks long.
4. Ali has two brothers and a sister.
5. It costs $49.50.
6. It is a hundred miles to San Diego.
7. The reading assignment is five pages long.
8. New York has a population of 8 million.
9. There are twelve students in the class.
10. She lives twelve blocks from the university.

**D2. Write three questions using *how* and an adjective.

E. Negative present perfect (S + *have/has* + *not* + past participle)

Put *not* between *have/has* and the past participle to make a present perfect sentence negative.

Glen *has finished* the assignment.
Glen *has not finished* the assignment.

E1. **Make each sentence negative.**

1. María has been to Paris.

2. They have found an apartment.

3. He has had breakfast this morning.

E2. **Write three negative sentences in the present perfect.

F. Already/yet

We often use *already* and *yet* with the present perfect. Use *already* with an affirmative sentence and *yet* with a negative sentence. Use either *already* or *yet* in questions. Put *yet* at the end of the sentence. Put *already* between *have/has* and the present participle.

Summary

already	yet
affirmative *have* + *already* + past participle questions	negative (sentence) *yet*. questions

Marie has been in Montreal for a month. She has *already* visited Quebec and Ottawa. She has not been to Toronto *yet* but she plans to go soon.

Already shows that something has happened. *Yet* shows that something has not happened but possibly will happen.

F1. **Add *already* or *yet* to each sentence.**

1. The program has not begun.

2. I have read that magazine.

3. Have you found an apartment?

4. She has been to Niagara Falls.

5. We have had a lot of bad weather and it is snowing again.

6. I have not spoken to her about the problem.

7. They have thought about it for a long time.

8. Has she learned to drive?

**F2.   Write two sentences with *already* and two with *yet.* Use the present perfect tense.

WRITE

A.   Interview someone in the class. Ask about what he/she has done since he/she started this English course. Ask questions like these:

> How long have you been here?
> What interesting things have you done?
> Have you made any new friends?
> Has anything funny or unpleasant happened to you?
> What are two things you have wanted to do but have not done yet?

Write a composition about the person's experiences.

B.   Use these expressions and underline them.

> 1. two negative present perfect sentences
> 2. *already*
> 3. *yet*
> 4. *for* or *since*

C.   Check your paper using numbers 10, 14, 17, and 18.

Future Plans

PRACTICE

A. Review

A1. Write the past and past participle for each verb.

understand	have
begin	ring
speak	read
hurt	let
tell	think
find	leave
drink	sing
hide	fight

A2. Write *much, many,* or *a lot of* in the blanks. Use *much* or *many* whenever it is possible.

1. The teacher has _____ information about places to visit here.
2. We have not had _____ good weather lately.
3. Are there _____ mountains in your country?
4. There are not _____ rivers.
5. Do you have _____ jewelry?
6. There is _____ traffic today.
7. Do you need to buy _____ food for the party?
8. My city has _____ high-rise buildings.
9. There are not _____ women in the class.
10. Do we have _____ homework for tomorrow?

A3. Rewrite this paragraph. Combine some of the sentences and add capital letters and punctuation.

mohammed is one of my classmates he is from saudi arabia he is a tall young man he has black curly hair and brown eyes he usually wears jeans and a shirt his favorite colors are green and blue mohammed likes to play soccer he is an intelligent student and studies hard every day he is a very nice person and all of the students like him

B. Future: will (S + *will* + SV)

1. *Will* means *be going to.* Use the simple verb without *to* after *will.*
   We *will have* a test tomorrow.
   Mary *will be* twenty years old next Tuesday.
2. Put *not* after *will* for the negative. (S + *will* + *not* + SV)
   We *will not* have a test tomorrow.
3. Put *will* before the subject for a question. (*will* + S + SV)
   Will we have a test tomorrow?

B1. Change each sentence to the future with *will.*

1. They are going to leave for Caracas next week.
2. Are they going to fly?
3. Betty is not in class.
4. Charles is going to go to the library this afternoon.
5. The Browns are not going to attend the concert after all.

6. The semester does not finish for two more weeks.

7. Marie is not going to buy a car after all.

8. Are you going to be home tonight?

**B2. Use *will* in an affirmative sentence, a negative sentence, and a question.

C. A few/a little

Use *a few* with count nouns and *a little* with noncount nouns. Do not use *a few* or *a little* in negative sentences.

> She has *a few* dollars in the bank.
> Does she have *a few* dollars in the bank?
> She has *a little* money in the bank.
> Does she have *a little* money in the bank?

C1. Fill in the blanks with *a few* or *a little*.

1. I have only _____ information about that university.

2. Would you like to listen to _____ music?

3. There is _____ coffee left in the pot.

4. I have _____ more sentences to write.

5. _____ students missed the picnic.

6. We have only _____ homework today.

7. _____ people were late yesterday.

8. She will buy _____ new clothes for winter.

9. I plan to visit _____ cities before I leave this country.

10. She wants only _____ salt on her food.

**C2. Write four sentences. Write an affirmative sentence and a question with *a few* and an affirmative sentence and a question with *a little*.

D. To be going to: questions (be + S + *going to* + SV, wh- word + *be* + S + *going to* + SV)

A yes/no question with *going to* has *be* before the subject. The wh- word is the first word in the sentence.

> Sam is going to buy a home computer.
> *Is* Sam *going to* buy a home computer?
> *What is* Sam *going to* buy?

D1. Change some statements to a yes/no question. If some words are in *italics*, change the statement to a wh- question.

1. She is going to have *some coffee*.
2. Tom is going to drive to Berlin.
3. They are going to think about it first.
4. The semester is going to start *in three weeks*.
5. They are going to help each other.
6. Liz is going to stop at the supermarket *on the way home tonight*.
7. Alice is going to leave early *because she has to do some errands*.
8. They are going to get married.

**D2. Write two yes/no and two wh- questions with *going to*.

E. Sentence combining: will/going to + when/until/before/after + present

Method 11

The part of the sentence with *when, until, before,* or *after* is in the present tense even when the real time is future.

I will give you the book.
I will see you tonight.
I *will give* you the book *when* I *see* you tonight.
She is going to study the verbs.
She will know them.
She *is going to study* the verbs *until* she *knows* them.
He will get a master's degree.
He will start looking for a job.
He *will get* a master's degree *before* he *starts* looking for a job.
I will finish my English course.
I will start on my Ph.D.
I *will start* on my Ph.D. after I *finish* my English course.

E1. Combine these pairs of sentences. Use the correct verb forms.

1. I will visit Los Angeles.   (before)

    I will go to San Francisco.
2. Paula is going to work part time.   (until)

    She will save $200.
3. She will stay in the United States.   (until)

    She will get her master's degree.

4. David will get a good job.   (when)

He will finish his English course.

5. I will learn English.   (after)

I will return to my job.

**E2.   Write four sentences like the ones in E. Use *when*, *until*, *before*, and *after*.

F.   Rewriting

This paragraph is correct but it could be much better. Write it again. Combine some sentences and make other changes to improve the composition.

MY CITY

My city is Culiacan. Culiacan is the capital of Sinaloa, Mexico. This city is very old. It is much older than Guadalajara. Near Culiacan there are many large farms. Many people in Culiacan are farmers. There are a lot of stores in the city. The farmers go shopping there. My city is not very big but it is very pleasant. It is not very difficult to make friends. Life in Culiacan is good.

WRITE

A.   What are your plans for the future? What will you do after you finish this English course? Will you study for a degree? What will you do after that? Will you get a job when you finish this course? Where are you going to live? Will you get married? Use these ideas and some of your own. Write a composition about your plans and hopes for the future.

B.   Use these expressions and underline them.

1. two sentences in the future tense combined with *when*
2. a negative sentence with *will*
3. *to be going to*

C.   Check your paper using numbers 10, 14, 17, and 18.

Lesson 23

Giving Advice

PRACTICE

A. Review

A1. Write an imperative sentence for each situation.

1. You should come to class on time.
2. You must think it over carefully before you decide.
3. Can you call me tonight?
4. Will you stop making that noise?
5. You must remember to bring your ticket.

A2. Write a sentence with a modal for each situation. (Use *will, can, may, might, should,* or *must.*)

1. Betty is going to leave tomorrow.

2. I advise you to hand in your homework on time.

3. Maybe she will wear a long dress to the party.

4. Go to the office immediately.

5. It is possible that John will fail the examination.

A3. Write the correct comparison form in the blank.

1. (young) David is _____ Bob.

2. (old) There are six people in my family. I am _____.

3. (beautiful) Diamonds are _____ glass.

4. (Tall) _____ building in the world is in Chicago.

5. (intelligent) Carmen is _____ student in the class.

6. (easy) Reading is _____ writing.

7. (beautiful) Cleopatra was _____ woman in the world.

8. (big) Tokyo is _____ city in Japan.

B. Modals: negatives and questions

Negatives: put *not* after a modal to form the negative. *Cannot* is one word. (S + modal + *not* + SV)

She *will not* be here tomorrow.
I *cannot* hear you.
They *may not* leave until next week.
We *might not* go to the party tonight.
Keiko *should not* worry about her grades.
Children *must not* play with matches.

B1. Change each sentence to the negative.

1. Glen might go to Indiana after all.

2. Jean can speak French.

3. Paul should help his brother do his homework.

4. We might see each other at the game tonight.

5. They may get to Boston tomorrow.

6. He will be on time for the meeting.

Questions: Put the modal before the subject to make a question. We do not usually use *might* in questions. We use *may* only when it means permission. (modal + S + SV)

May I smoke in the hall?
Should we call for reservations before we leave?
Must we do it?

B2. Change each statement to a question.

1. Paul can play the violin.

2. I may leave class early.

3. Your brother should fill out these papers.

4. Carol will take the test next week.

5. We must go.

**B3. Write two questions and two negative sentences with modals.

C. Imperatives: negatives (*do not* + SV)

Put *do not* or *don't* before all verbs, including *be*. (There is no subject in an imperative sentence.)

Be careful when you write verb forms.
Do not be careless.
Connect two sentences with *and*.
Do not connect two sentences with a comma.

C1. Change each sentence to the negative imperative. Use *do not* or *don't*.

1. You should not begin a sentence with *because*.

2. You should not use abbreviations in compositions.

3. You must be quiet in your laboratory class.

4. You cannot use your dictionary during a quiz.

5. You should not put an -*s* on adjectives.

6. You must not forget the title.

7. You must not copy from someone else's paper.

**C2. Write three negative imperative sentences.

D. One, another one, the other one

1.   *One* is a substitute for a noun with an indefinite article (a, an).
     Peter has *a blue jacket* and Howard has *one* too.

2.   *Another one* means *different* or *additional.* It is indefinite.
     My brother wants to go to this restaurant but I want to go to *another one.* (There are several restaurants.)
     Mary already has a raincoat but she is going to buy *another one.*

3.   *The other one* shows that there are only two.
     My brother wants to eat at this cafeteria but I want to eat at *the other one.* (There are only two cafeterias in the Student Union.)
     Mary likes this raincoat but she likes *the other one* better. (She is choosing between two raincoats.)

4.   Use *the other ones* for a plural noun.
     She likes this raincoat but she does not like *the other ones.* (There are several in the store.)
     There are four restaurants at the Student Union. One has waiters and *the other ones* are cafeterias.

D1. Put *one, another one, the other one,* or *the other ones* in the blanks.

1.   Paul has a used car but Sarah has a new _____one_____.

2.   We have four exercises for homework. One is hard but
     ___the other ones___ are easy.

3.   I have already had two cups of coffee. I do not want ___another___.

4.   There are still two tapes that nobody picked up. _____ is
     Helen's. Whose is _____?

5.   The child ate a piece of cake and then asked for ___another one___.

6.   Keiko has a bilingual dictionary. Do you have _____?

7.   The name of one of the twins is Paul. _____ is Paula.

8.   They had a test Friday and they will have _____ tomorrow.

**D2.   Use *one, another one, the other one,* and *the other ones* in sentences.

E. Adverbials of purpose (V + *to* + V, V + *for* + N)

Sometimes we answer the question *why* with the answer *because.* . . . We can also use an adverbial of purpose. Use *to* and a verb or *for* and a noun.

Why is Masako studying tonight?
She is studying *because* she has a test tomorrow.
She is studying *to pass* a test tomorrow.
She is studying *for a test* tomorrow.

Why did Don go shopping?
He went *because* he needed some groceries.
He went *to buy* some groceries.
He went *for* some groceries.

E1.   Finish each sentence.

1. Robert went to the supermarket to

2. Pam went to the bookstore for

3. Betty is studying English to

4. Marie went to Vancouver to

5. Tony came to my apartment for

6. Jean wrote to her parents to

7. Carlos left early to

8. We went to the mall for

9. I turned on the television to

10. Sarah got up early to

**E2.   Write two sentences with a verb showing purpose and two with a noun showing purpose.

F. Capitalize and punctuate the following composition. Put the paragraph symbol (¶) to show where the second and third paragraphs start. Do not copy the composition. Just write in the capital letters and punctuation.

MASAKO

masako is a japanese student at the university of arizona she is from tokyo and she wants to learn english because she works for a large company this is masakos first semester she has six classes but they do not all meet every day her first class is at eight oclock and then she has a free period she usually goes to the student union for breakfast when she has free time in the afternoon she goes to the library to do her homework she also studies several evenings a week sometimes when all of her homework is done she goes to a movie she has attended two concerts and one football game next year she wants to learn how to swim if she has time she likes living in tucson but she is disappointed because she has not met many americans

WRITE

A. A friend or relative has a problem. It might be a serious one or maybe it is not very important. Think of a problem and then write a letter giving advice and suggestions about this problem. Use modals and imperatives.

B. Use these expressions and underline them.

1. a negative modal
2. a negative imperative
3. *one, another one, the other one,* or *the other ones*

C. Check your paper using numbers 10, 14, 17, and 18.

A Special Vacation

PRACTICE

A. Review

A1. Make a sentence from each group of words. Add any necessary words and use the correct verb forms.

1. never / they / winter / take / trip

2. usually / not / I / go out / Monday / night

3. sometimes / George / stay up / late / night

4. always / not / she / come / class

5. seldom / Ruth / spend / Sunday / library

A2. **Make a question or a negative sentence from each group of words. Add any necessary words.**

1. could / not / he / come / my party / night
2. will / they / sightseeing / their vacation
3. must / not / you / be / late
4. should / she / long dress / party
5. can / not / Bill / get / airport / time

A3. **Each sentence has one mistake. Find it and correct it.**

WRONG

1. I got your last letter. When you told me about your problem.
2. I am waiting for your phone call for two weeks.
3. Do you want another ones tomorrow?
4. You should try to found someone to share your apartment.
5. He has arrived three months ago.
6. One day she waited a long time for her husband, he was late.
7. He met some airports on his way here.
8. She has to after that call her cousin.
9. She has done a lot of new friends here.
10. But one day when we were riding on the motorcycle, we had an accident.

B. **Adverbs of frequency: questions (always, usually, often, sometimes, seldom, rarely, never) (be + S + *always*, *do/does* + S + *always*)**

1. Put *always* or *usually* after the subject in a question.
   Are you *usually* home on Sunday?
   Does she *always* talk a lot?
2. *Often* is usually at the end of a question.
   Do you go there *often*?
3. We do not usually use *sometimes, seldom, rarely,* or *never* in a question.
4. We often use *ever* in a question. The question means the same without *ever*.
   Does she ride her bicycle to school?
   Does she *ever* ride her bicycle to school?
5. Put *always, usually,* or *ever* after *is/are there.*
   Is there *usually* a quiz on Friday?

B1. Add the adverb of frequency to the questions.

1. (ever)　Do you go to the beach on your vacation?
2. (always)　Does he get up early?
3. (often)　Do they go swimming?
4. (usually)　Is there a lot of traffic on this street?
5. (ever)　Did you meet Carol?
6. (always)　Are there red marks on your compositions?
7. (usually)　Does Mary wear a dress to parties?
8. (often)　Do you go out?

**B2. Write three questions with adverbs of frequency. Use *ever* in one of them.

C. Adverbs of frequency with modals (S + modal + *always*)

1. Put the adverb of frequency after the modal in a statement:
   You must *never* do that again.
2. Put the adverb of frequency after *not*.
   I cannot *always* take you to the university in my car.
3. Put the adverb of frequency after the subject in a question. We often use *ever* in questions.
   Will you *ever* learn to write perfect compositions?

C1. Add the adverb of frequency to the sentences.

1. (ever)　Should you copy someone's paper?
2. (never)　I can thank you enough.
3. (often)　Will you think of me?
4. (always)　She will remember her college friends.
5. (ever)　Will you visit my country?
6. (never)　I will come back to this restaurant.

**C2. Write two sentences with both an adverb of frequency and a modal.

D. Adverbs of frequency with present perfect (*have/has* + *always* + past participle)

Put the adverb of frequency between *have/has* and the past participle.

She *has never been* to France.

Put the adverb of frequency after the subject in a question. We often use *ever* in present perfect questions.

Have you *always* lived in a big house?
Have you *ever* been to France?

D1.   Add the adverb of frequency to the sentences.

1.   (ever)   Have you traveled by ship?
2.   (always)   She has gotten good grades.
3.   (never)   She has gone to a rock concert.
4.   (ever)   Has Bob studied calculus?
5.   (seldom)   She has come to class late before but she is late today.
6.   (usually)   I have lived in an apartment but now I am living in a dormitory.

**D2.   Write three sentences using an adverb of frequency with the present perfect.

E.   Another, the other, the others

It is not always necessary to write *another one*, *the other one*, or *the other ones*. *Another*, *the other*, or *the others* are also correct.

She already has a raincoat but she is going to buy *another one*.
She already has a raincoat but she is going to buy *another*.
You like this car but I like *the other one* better.
You like this car but I like *the other* better.
Three students in the class are Japanese.
The other ones are Europeans.
The others are Europeans.

E1.   Put *another*, *the other*, or *the others* in the blanks.

1.   We have four exercises for homework. One is hard but
     _____ are easy.
2.   I have already had two cups of coffee. I do not want _____.
3.   One of these papers is Mary's. Whose is _____?
4.   Dan had a cup of coffee and then asked for _____.
5.   The name of one of the twins is Paul. _____ is Paula.
6.   They had a test Friday and they will have _____ tomorrow.

**E2.   Use *another*, *the other*, and *the others* in sentences.

F. Add periods and capital letters to this paragraph. Put the paragraph symbol (¶) where a new paragraph should start. Do not copy the paragraph.

los angeles is a large city in california when you go there be prepared to see lots of cars there are thousands of cars going about ten miles an hour during the busiest hours but traffic is not very bad in the middle of the day hollywood is a very famous part of los angeles it used to be the center of the american movie industry but today the movie studios are in other parts of the city you can tour some of the movie studios and see some of the homes of famous movie stars los angeles has interesting museums good restaurants and beautiful beaches it is a good place to spend a vacation

WRITE

A. You are going to take a special vacation and have all the money you want to spend. You can do anything or go anywhere you like. What would you like to do? Describe your vacation. Use modals in most sentences.

B. Use these expressions and underline them.

1. the present perfect tense
2. an adverb of frequency
3. two sentences combined with *because*

C. Check your paper using numbers 10, 14, 17, and 18.

A Letter to Myself

PRACTICE

A. Review

A1. Write a sentence with *used to* for each situation.

1. I lived in an apartment when I was a child.
2. My aunt traveled in Europe every summer.
3. Jim played with his friends every Saturday.
4. Peter was never on time for anything but he has changed.
5. My mother went shopping every weekend.
6. I always thought English was hard.

A2. Write *very* or *too* in the blanks.

1. She spoke _____ fast for me to understand.
2. I thought the concert was _____ good.
3. We have _____ much homework. I do not have time to do it.
4. The police officer gave Howard a ticket because he was driving _____ fast.
5. We will have to leave _____ early in the morning.

A3. Write the past and past participle of each verb.

find	break
catch	mean
think	stand
keep	build
sell	ring
fight	know
let	win
wear	ride

B. Irregular verbs

Learn these verb forms.

Simple Form	Past	Past Participle
cut	cut	cut
put	put	put
cost	cost	cost
throw	threw	thrown
fly	flew	flown
blow	blew	blown
choose	chose	chosen
bring	brought	brought
give	gave	given
sit	sat	sat
steal	stole	stolen
fall	fell	fallen

B1. Write the correct verb form in the blanks.

1. Did you _____ the milk in the refrigerator?
2. Karl has _____ a friend to class today.
3. Marie _____ away her old shoes last week.

4. Dan has not _____ his major yet.

5. They _____ in the front row because they wanted to hear everything.

6. Helen _____ the cake in sixteen pieces.

7. My sister _____ to Manila last week.

8. Someone has _____ my wallet!

9. The wind _____ hard last night.

10. Have you ever _____ a speech in class?

11. David _____ off his bicycle and broke his leg.

12. It _____ $170 to have my car repaired last month.

**B2.   Use four of the verbs in sentences in the past or present perfect.

C.   Reflexive pronouns (-self pronouns)

When you look in the mirror, you see your reflection. A mirror reflects. Reflexive pronouns reflect on the subject of the sentence.

You see *yourself* in the mirror.
The child cut *herself* by accident.
I do not need any help. I can do it by *myself*.

Subject Pronoun	Reflexive Pronoun
I	myself
you	yourself
he	himself
she	herself
it	itself
we	ourselves
you	yourselves
they	themselves

Most reflexive pronouns use the possessive pronoun and *-self* or *-selves*. *Himself* and *themselves* use the object forms.

C1.   Put a reflexive pronoun in each blank.

1. Mr. Johnson bought a shirt for his son and one for _____.

2. You should talk about this among _____.

3. With some cameras you can take a picture of _____.

4. The Franks' small daughter fell down and hurt _____.

5. I chose a green T-shirt for _____ and a blue one for my sister.

6. A cat can find food for _____.

7. Children should learn to do things by _____.

8. Put _____ in his place. Think how he feels.

9. We looked at _____ in the mirror.

C2. **Use four reflexive pronouns in sentences.

D. Useful expressions

be interested in (+ N)	instead of
be interested in (+ V-ing)	in a hurry
old friends	make a mistake
after all	be proud of
change your mind	

D1. Fill in the blanks.

1. We have known each other since we were children. We are

   _____.

2. Barbara was going to study nutrition _____ chemical engineering. Then she changed her mind.

3. She is not going to study chemical engineering _____.

4. Carol is interested _____ sports.

5. I am interested in (visit) _____ Niagara Falls.

6. Peter never slows down. He is always _____.

7. Robert is _____ himself because he got an A on his quiz.

8. I am not going to the beach after all. I changed _____.

9. I _____ three mistakes on the quiz yesterday.

D2. **Use six of the expressions in sentences. Choose ones that are new to you.

E. Prepositions + V-ing (prep + N, prep + V-ing)

A preposition usually has a noun or *V-ing* after it. The *V-ing* is the noun form of the verb. When we use *V-ing* as a noun, we call it a *gerund*. (*To* is different because it often has the simple verb after it. There are also some two-word verbs that must have a simple verb instead of a gerund.)

I am thinking *about buying* a new car.
She is interested *in studying* chemistry.
We are going to stay here instead *of flying* to Europe.
You can improve your English *by watching* television.
We use a stove *for cooking*.
I look forward *to seeing* you.

E1.   Finish each sentence.

1. I am interested in
2. I want to _____ instead of
3. I look forward to
4. I am thinking about
5. You can lose weight by
6. We use a _____ for

**E2.   Write six sentences using a preposition and a gerund.

WRITE

A.   Write a letter to yourself. Think about what you have done this semester. Tell what you are proud of and tell how you want to change yourself. You may want to give yourself advice.

B.   Use these expressions and underline them.

1. two irregular verbs from B
2. a reflexive pronoun
3. two of the expressions from D
4. *too* or *very*

C.   Correct your paper using numbers 10, 14, 17, and 18.

Grammar
Reference Section

VERBS

Every sentence must have a verb in it.

Present Tense

Affirmative

Use the present tense to describe a habitual or repeated action (something you always or usually do). Use it also to give general information.

I usually *get up* at 7:00 in the morning.
He often *plays* soccer on Sunday.

I *visit* my family every vacation.
Tom *is* a student.
I *like* to watch television.
The Earth *is* round.

Use the *s* form of the verb with all singular subjects except *I* and *you*.

Be is irregular: is
Have is irregular: has

Bill usually *gets up* early.
He *has* a big breakfast.
Mary *leaves* for the university at 7:30 a.m.
She *arrives* at the university at 8:00.
My cat *is* brown.
It *likes* to sleep a lot.
My car *has* a flat tire.
The Student Union *opens* at 7:00 a.m.

Use the simple form of the verb with *I, you,* and all plural subjects. *Be* is irregular: am/are

They never *come* to class late.
Mr. and Mrs. Baker *leave* for home at 5:00 p.m.
The students *practice* their English between classes.
You *are* all good students.
I usually *have* lunch in the cafeteria.
You *are* a good student.

I play	we play
you play	you play
he plays	
she plays	they play
it plays	

The verb *be* is irregular.

I am	we are
you are	you are
he is	
she is	they are
it is	

The verb *have* is irregular.

I have	we have
you have	you have
he has	
she has	they have
it has	

The spelling of *go* and *do* is irregular.

I go   he goes, she goes, it goes
I do   he does, she does, it does

Negative

Put *not* after *be* to make a negative sentence in the present tense.

She is busy.
She is *not* busy.

Put *do/does not* before the simple verb to form the negative of other verbs.

I watch television in the evening.
I *do not watch* television in the evening.
He has breakfast at home.
He *does not have* breakfast at home.

Questions with be

Put *be* before the subject in a yes/no question. (See page 165.)

　Her name is Mary.
Is her name Mary?
　Tom is a student.
Is Tom a student?

Put the *wh-* word at the beginning in a *wh-* question. (See page 165.)

　　Her name is Mary.
　Is her name Mary?
What is her name?

Questions with other verbs

Use *do/does* with the simple verb in a yes/no question with other verbs.

　You live in a dormitory.
Do you *live* in a dormitory?
　Tom goes to class every day.
Does Tom *go* to class every day?

Put the *wh-* word at the beginning of the sentence in a *wh-* question. (See page 165.)

　　You live in a dormitory.
　Do you *live* in a dormitory?
Where do you *live*?

There is/There are

Affirmative

Use a singular noun or a noncount noun after *there is*. Then use *it* in the second sentence.

There is a small *garden* behind my house. *It* has flowers and vegetables.
There is a lot of *food* in the refrigerator. *It* is for a party.

Use a plural noun after *there are*. Then use *they*.

There are three *bedrooms* in my house. *They* are on the second floor.

Negative

Put *not* after *is* or *are*.

There *isn't* any food in the refrigerator.
There *aren't* any Germans in my class.

Questions

Put *is* or *are* before *there* for a question.

Is there any milk in the refrigerator?
Are there any Germans in your class?

Imperatives

Affirmative

Use the imperative form (the simple verb) to tell someone to do something. Use it to give an order or make a request (ask someone to do something).

There is no subject in an imperative sentence. We understand that the subject is *you* but we do not write it or say it.

Please makes the sentence more polite. Use it for requests.

Please close the door.
Study the new lesson for tomorrow.
Do the exercises for homework.

Negative

We use *do not* with the simple verb and no subject to make a negative imperative sentence.

Please *do not close* the door.
Do not study the new lesson for tomorrow.
Do not do the exercises for homework.

Questions

There are no imperative questions.

Past Tense

Affirmative

Use the past tense to describe a completed action, an action that is completely finished.

I *walked* to class yesterday.
He *lived* in France from 1975 to 1980.
They *were* at a party last night.

Add *-ed* to regular verbs to form the past tense. If the verb ends in *-e*, just add *-d*. There is no *-s* form in the past tense.

walk	walked	live	lived
brush	brushed	use	used

See page 167 for spelling rules.

Some verbs have irregular forms in the past tense. You must memorize them. See the list of irregular verbs on page 148.

Negative

Use *not* with the past tense of *be* for the negative form. Write *not* after *was* or *were*.

We *were not* at home last weekend.
He *was not* in class yesterday.

Use *did not* with the simple verb for the negative form of the past tense of other verbs.

I *did not* walk to class yesterday. I came by bus.
He *did not go* to Washington last weekend because he was sick.

Questions

Past tense questions with *be* are like present tense questions but we use the past tense of *be* (*was/were*).

She was at the beach yesterday
Was she at the beach yesterday?
Where was she yesterday?
Who was at the beach yesterday?

Past tense questions with other verbs are also like present tense questions but we use the past tense of *do (did)*. Use the simple form of the other verb.

> He went to Japan last summer.
> *Did he go* to Japan last summer?
> *Where did he go* last summer?
> *Who went* to Japan last summer?

Present Continuous Tense

Affirmative

Use the present continuous for something that is happening right now.

I *am sitting* in class now.
My brother *is studying* in New York this year.

Use the present tense of *be (am, is, are)* and the *-ing* form (present participle) of another verb for the present continuous tense.

We *are studying* English now.
The teacher *is explaining* the lesson now.

See page 167 for spelling rules.

Negative

Put *not* after *be* to form the negative.

My brother *is not* studying in New York this year.

Questions

Put *be* before the subject to form a question. The *wh-* word is the first word in the sentence.

> The teacher is explaining the lesson.
> *Is* the teacher explaining the lesson?
> *What* is the teacher explaining?
> *Who* is explaining the lesson?

Past Continuous Tense

Affirmative

Use the past continuous tense to describe a continuous action in the past. We often use the past continuous to show that one action interrupted another. Use the simple past for the action that interrupted something.

I *was eating* dinner when the phone *rang.*
They were talking to each other when I *interrupted* them.

The past continuous is like the present continuous but we use the past tense of
be (was/were).
Tom *was studying* when his friend knocked at the door.
They *were watching* television when the electricity went off.

Negative

Put *not* after *was/were.*

You did not interrupt us. We *were not doing* anything when you called.

Questions

Put *was/were* before the subject. The *wh-* word is the first word in the sentence.

Were you doing something when I called you?
What were you doing when I called you?

Be Going To (Future)

Affirmative

Use *be going to* with the simple verb for future time.

I *am going to visit* my uncle next week.
Nadia *is going to take* the TOEFL test in two weeks.
We *are going to go* to London next summer.

Negatives

Put *not* after *be* in a negative sentence.

I *am not* going to visit my uncle next week.
Nadia *is not* going to take the TOEFL test in two weeks.
We *are not* going to go to London next summer.

Questions

Put *be* before the subject in a yes/no question. The *wh-* word is the first word in
the sentence.

Sam is going to buy a home computer.
Is Sam going to buy a home computer?
What is Sam going to buy?

Will (Future)

Affirmative

Use *will* with the simple verb for future time. There is no *to* after *will*.

We *will have* a test tomorrow.
Mary *will be* twenty years old next Tuesday.

Negative

Put *not* after *will* for the negative.

We *will not* have a test tomorrow.

Questions

Put *will* before the subject for a question.

Will we have a test tomorrow?

Present Perfect Tense

Affirmative

The present perfect tense shows that an action or condition started in the past, is continuing now, and will probably continue into the future. When the person thinks about this action or condition, she/he connects the past action to the present time. He/she sees a connection between the past and the present. The action or condition is probably not finished yet. Maybe the person will continue or repeat the action or condition.

Mary *has been* here for two months. (She came in January. Now it is March and she is still here. She will probably be here for several months.)

Since I arrived I *have gone* to two shopping centers, an interesting museum, and a large park. (I will be here for two years and I will probably visit many more places.)

Tony *has taken* twenty pictures this week. (Today is Thursday. Tony started taking pictures on Monday. The week is not finished and he might take some more pictures.)

Use *have/has* with the past participle for the present perfect tense.

I *have lived* here for six years.
Mary *has studied* English for three years.
David *has played* the piano since he was a child.
He *has been* to New York three times.

Past participles

The past participle is the third form of verbs.

In regular verbs, the past participle is the same as the past tense form. Add *-ed* to the simple verb.

Simple Form	Past	Past Participle
talk	talked	talked
listen	listened	listened

You must memorize the past participle of irregular verbs. See page 148 for a list of irregular verbs.

Negative

Put *not* after *have/has* in a negative present perfect sentence.

Glen has finished the assignment.
Glen *has not* finished the assignment.

Questions

Put the subject after *have/has* to make a yes/no question in the present perfect. The wh- word is the first word in the sentence.

She has been at the Student Union all morning.
Has she been at the Student Union all morning?
Where has she been all morning?

(See *already/yet* and *for/since* on page 164.)

Used To

Affirmative

We often use *used to* to show habitual action in the past. Use the simple verb after *used to*.

When I was a child, I *used to* play with my friends all the time.
Pat *used to* study a lot when she was in high school.

Negative

Use *did + not + use to* for negative sentences.

She *did not use to* study very much, but now she does.

Questions

Use *did* + *use to* for questions.

Did you *use to* study much when you were in high school?

Verb + to + Verb

Some verbs have *to* after them if the next word is a verb. Always use the simple form of the second verb. These are some common verbs followed by *to*:

agree to	need to
decide to	plan to
expect to	prepare to
forget to	promise to
have to (must)	remember to
hope to	want to
learn to	try to

I *want to go* to the basketball game tonight.
He *tried to call* you last night but the line was busy.
I *have to study* for a test tomorrow. (I must study.)
I usually go right home after class but today I *decided to go* shopping.

Irregular Verbs

Simple Form	Past	Past Participle
be	was/were	been
begin	began	begun
bite	bit	bitten
break	broke	broken
bring	brought	brought
buy	bought	bought
catch	caught	caught
choose	chose	chosen
come	came	come
cost	cost	cost
cut	cut	cut
do	did	done
drink	drank	drunk
drive	drove	driven
eat	ate	eaten
fall	fell	fallen
feel	felt	felt
fight	fought	fought
find	found	found
fly	flew	flown
forget	forgot	forgotten (forgot)
get	got	gotten (got)
give	gave	given
go	went	gone
grow	grew	grown
have	had	had
hear	heard	heard

Simple Form	Past	Past Participle
hit	hit	hit
hold	held	held
hurt	hurt	hurt
keep	kept	kept
know	knew	known
let	let	let
lie	lay	lain
light	lit	lit
lose	lost	lost
make	made	made
mean	meant	meant
meet	met	met
pay	paid	paid
put	put	put
read	read	read
ride	rode	ridden
ring	rang	rung
run	ran	run
say	said	said
see	saw	seen
sell	sold	sold
send	sent	sent
shut	shut	shut
sing	sang	sung
sit	sat	sat
sleep	slept	slept
speak	spoke	spoken
spend	spent	spent
stand	stood	stood
steal	stole	stolen
swim	swam	swum
take	took	taken
teach	taught	taught
tell	told	told
think	thought	thought
throw	threw	thrown
understand	understood	understood
wake	woke	waked (woken)
wear	wore	worn
win	won	won
write	wrote	written

MODALS

Affirmative

Use the simple verb after a modal. Never use *to* after a modal. Some modals have two meanings.

will	= be going to	may	= maybe
can	= be able to	might	= maybe
can	= permission	should	= advice
may	= permission	must	= have to

She *will* arrive tomorrow.
He *can* sing very well.
You *can* smoke in the hall but not in the classroom.
You *may* smoke in the hall.
I *may* go to the movies tonight but I am not sure.
I *might* go to the movies tonight but I am not sure.
You *should* study the irregular verbs. You have five of them wrong.
You *must* improve your grades or you will fail this course.

Negative

Put *not* after a modal to form the negative. *Cannot* is one word.

She will *not* be here tomorrow.
I *cannot* hear you.
They may *not* leave until next week.
We might *not* go to the party tonight.
Keiko should *not* worry about her grades.
Children must *not* play with matches.

Questions

Put the modal before the subject to make a question. We do not usually use *might* in questions. We use *may* only when it means permission.

May I smoke in the hall?
Should we call for reservations before we leave?
Must we do it?

Could

Could is the past tense of *can* when it means ability. (It also has some other uses.)

Tom *can* run ten kilometers.
Tom *could* run five kilometers last year.
George *cannot* run ten kilometers.
George *could not* run ten kilometers last year either.

Like to/would like to

Would like to means *want to*. Use it for the future.

I *would like to* visit Hawaii.
(I want to visit Hawaii.)
Would you *like to* go to the basketball game tonight?
(Do you want to go to the basketball game tonight?)

Like to tells an opinion or information.

She *likes to* watch television.
He *liked to* play soccer when he was a child.

NOUNS

A noun is the name of a person, place, thing, or idea. These are examples of nouns:

Mary	London	pencil	love
Mr. Brown	Pacific Ocean	shirt	happiness
child	Japan	apple	beauty

Count and noncount nouns

We can count some things. These are count nouns. A count noun has a plural form. It can have a number in front of it. (See page 166 for spelling rules for plural forms.)

a building	two buildings
a dollar	six dollars
a room	four rooms

We cannot count some things. These are noncount nouns. (*Non-* means *no* or *not*.) A noncount noun does not have a plural form and it cannot have a number in front of it. These are some common noncount nouns:

water	food	cheese	meat
coffee	fruit	rice	ham
tea	bread	salt	chicken
milk	toast	pepper	beef
juice	butter	soup	pork
ice cream	bacon	fish	

chalk	homework	traffic	weather
furniture	vocabulary	transportation	rain
soap	money	love	snow
music	information	beauty	wind
luggage	jewelry	happiness	air
baggage	work	fun	

We often put an indefinite article (*a, an*) before a count noun.

a woman	an apple	a tree

Use *an* before a word that begins with a vowel *sound.*

an *apple*	an *Indian*	an *umbrella*
an *elephant*	an *old* house	an *hour*
	BUT: a (y)university	

We often put *some* before a noncount noun.

some furniture   some coffee   some soap

We often put *some* before a plural count noun too.

some chairs   some buildings   some rooms

Summary

Count	Noncount
singular and plural	no plural
singular: *a, an* plural: numbers, *some*	*some*
a banana an orange two chairs five dollars some sentences	some fruit some orange juice some furniture some money some homework

Possessive forms ('s, s')

Use *'s* (apostrophe *s*) with the names of people or animals to show possession.

1. Add *'s* to a singular noun.
    Jane's car is in the garage.
    A *giraffe's* neck is very long.
2. Add only an apostrophe to a plural noun. A plural noun already has an *-s*.
    The *girl's* coat is in the closet.
    The *girls'* coats are in the closet.
3. Some irregular plural nouns do not end in *-s*. Add *'s* to both singular and plural forms.

the *child's* toy	the *woman's* car	the *man's* desk
the *children's* toys	the *women's* cars	the *men's* desk

4. Use *of* with things to show possession.

the leaves *of* the tree	the roof *of* the house
the color *of* his shirt	the cover *of* the book

NOUN SUBSTITUTES

One is a substitute for a noun with an indefinite article (*a, an*).

Peter has *a blue jacket* and Howard has *one* too.

Another one means *different* or *additional*. It is indefinite.

My brother wants to go to this restaurant but I want to go to *another one*.
(There are several restaurants. My brother wants to go to one of them. I want to go to a different one.)

Mary already has a raincoat but she is going to buy *another one*. (There are a lot of raincoats in the stores. Mary will buy one of them.)

The other one shows that there are only two. It is definite.

My brother wants to eat at this cafeteria but I want to eat at *the other one*. (There are only two cafeterias in the Student Union.)
Mary likes this raincoat but she likes *the other one* better. (She is choosing between two raincoats.)

Use *the other ones* for a plural noun.

She likes this raincoat but she does not like *the other ones*. (There are several in the store.)
There are four restaurants at the Student Union. One has waiters and *the other ones* are cafeterias.

It is not always necessary to write *another one, the other one,* or *the other ones. Another, the other,* or *the others* are also correct.
She already has a raincoat but she is going to buy *another one*.
She already has a raincoat but she is going to buy *another*.
You like this car but I like *the other one* better.
You like this car but I like *the other* better.
Three students in the class are Japanese.
The other ones are Europeans.
The others are Europeans.

ARTICLES

A, an, and *the* are articles.

Indefinite

The indefinite articles are *a* and *an*. Use *a/an* before a singular noun.
Use *an* before a word that begins with a vowel *sound*.

an apple	an old house
an elephant	an umbrella
an Indian	

a university (the first *sound* is *y*)
an hour (the *h* is silent so the first *sound* is a vowel)

Use *a/an* when you write or speak about a noun for the first time. *A/an* before a noun shows that a person is a member of a general class or kind of people. *A/an* shows that a place or thing is one of a general class of places or things.

Mary is *an* engineer. (Mary is one of all the engineers in the world.)
Montreal is *a* city. (It is one of the many cities in the world.)
I went to *a* party last night. (There are many parties. I went to one of them.)

Use *a/an* before a singular noun.	Montreal is *a city.*
Use *a/an* before an adjective and a noun.	Montreal is *a large city.*
Do not use *a/an* before an adjective alone.	Montreal is *large.*

Your sister is *a child*.
Your sister is *a beautiful child*.
Your sister is *beautiful*.

Do not use *a/an* before a plural noun.
Do not use *a/an* before a noncount noun.

Cars are expensive.
Fruit is good for you.

Definite

The definite article is *the*.

You can use *the* with all kinds of nouns—singular and plural, count and noncount: the apple, the apples, the fruit.

Use *the* when both the writer and reader (or speaker and listener) are thinking about the same thing or person.

The cafeteria is closed today.
    (the cafeteria where we always eat)
I want to visit *the* art museum.
    (the art museum on campus)
The teacher gave us a lot of homework today.
    (the teacher of the class we finished five minutes ago)

Use *the* if the noun is already identified in the sentence before.

I had to study for *a test* last weekend. *The* test was hard.
There are *two large tables* in our classroom. *The* tables are in the back of the room.

Use *the* if the noun is identified by a phrase after the noun.

The tables *in our classroom* are large.
The homework *for today* was easy.

Do not use *the* with a noun used in a general way.

People must have *food* and *water*.
Water is necessary for all living things.
Susan is studying *history*.
Peter likes *coffee*.

Use *the* with a general noun if a phrase identifies it.

The people in my class are from five different countries.
The water *in this glass* is warm.
Susan is studying *the* history *of Japan*.
Peter does not like *the* coffee *in the student cafeteria*.

A few countries have *the* in the name.

the United States
the Union of Soviet Socialist Republics (the USSR)
the United Arab Emirates
the Netherlands
the Philippines

ADJECTIVES

An adjective describes a noun. Put the adjective before the noun.

a *large* house	a *small* garden
my *new* car	*brown* eyes

Put an adjective after *be*.

My house is *large*.	The garden is *small*.
My car is *new*.	His eyes are *brown*.

An adjective does not have a plural form.

a *large* house	a *new* car
three *large* houses	five *new* cars

Comparisons

We use adjectives to compare two people or things.
When an adjective has one syllable, add *-er* and use *than*.

Ann is *taller than* Paul.
My car is *older than* yours.

When an adjective has two syllables and ends in *y*, add *-er* and use *than*.

Spanish is *easier than* French.
Sarah is *prettier than* Marie.

Spelling: Use the *y* rule and the 1–1–1 rule before *-er*.

busy busier		big bigger

Use *more than* with adjectives that have three or more syllables.

Houses are usually *more expensive than* apartments.
Tony is *more intelligent than* Frank.

Good and *bad* are irregular.

Chocolate ice cream is *good*.
Strawberry ice cream is *better*.
Tom is a *bad* student.
Peter is a *worse* student than Tom.

Superlatives

We use the superlative form to compare three or more people or things.
When an adjective has one syllable, add *-est* and use *the*.

Tom is *tall*.
Paul is *taller than* Tom.
Bill is *the tallest* of the three men.

When an adjective has two syllables and ends in *-y*, add *-est* and use *the*.

French is *easy*.
Spanish is *easier than* French.
English is *the easiest* language in the world.

Spelling: Use the *y* rule and the 1–1–1 rule before *-est*.

busy   busier   busiest   big   bigger   biggest

Use *the most* with adjectives that have three or more syllables.

Ottawa is a *beautiful* city.
Rio de Janeiro is *more beautiful* than Ottawa.
My city is *the most beautiful* city in the world.

Good and *bad* are irregular.

Chocolate ice cream is *good*.
Strawberry ice cream is *better*.
Vanilla ice cream is *the best*.

Tom is a *bad* student.
Peter is a *worse* student *than* Tom.
Bill is *the worst* student in the class.

Summary

	1 syllable*	2 syllables -y*	2 or more syllables	good	bad
Comparative (2 things)	adj + -er than	adj + -er than	*more* adj than	better	worse
Superlative (3 or more things)	*the* adj + -est	*the* adj + -est	*the most* adj	best	worst

*Spelling: Use the *y* and the 1–1–1 rules.

Some/Any

Use *some* with affirmative statements. Use *any* with negative statements.
Use both *some* and *any* with questions.

Do you have *some* French stamps in your collection?
Do you have *any* French stamps in your collection?
My older brother has *some* French stamps but I do *not* have *any*.

Many/Much/A lot of

Use *many* with count nouns and *much* with noncount nouns. Use *a lot of* with both.

Use *many* and *much* with questions and negatives. Use *a lot of* with all kinds of sentences.

New York has *a lot of* high-rise buildings.   (count)
There are *not many* tall buildings in small cities.
Are there *many* modern buildings in Baghdad?
There is *a lot of* traffic during rush hours.   (noncount)
Is there *much* traffic on the side streets?
There is *not much* traffic at 2:00 a.m.

A few/A little

Use *a few* with count nouns and *a little* with noncount nouns. Do not use *a few* or *a little* in negative sentences.

She has *a few* dollars in the bank.   (count)
Does she have *a few* dollars in the bank?
She has *a little* money in the bank.   (noncount)
Does she have *a little* money in the bank?

Summary

	Count	Noncount
Affirmative	a lot of a few	a lot of a little
Negative	many a lot of	much a lot of
Questions	many a lot of a few	much a lot of a little

PRONOUNS

Subject	Object	Possessive Adjective (with a noun)	Possessive Pronoun (without a noun)	Reflexive
I	me	my	mine	myself
you	you	your	yours	yourself
he	him	his	his	himself
she	her	her	hers	herself
it	it	its	its	itself
we	us	our	ours	ourselves
you	you	your	yours	yourselves
they	them	their	theirs	themselves

Pronouns take the place of nouns.

Mary gave *her pencil* to *Tom.*
She gave *it* to *him.*

Subject pronouns

Use a subject pronoun as the subject of a sentence.

He called me last night.
They are studying English in London.
We like to go swimming in the afternoon.

Possessive adjectives

Possessive adjectives show that something belongs to someone.

That is Susan's car.
That is *her* car.

Use possessive adjectives with a noun.

His family lives in Caracas.
Her mother works for a large company.

Possessives have the same form with a singular or plural noun.

My shirt is in the closet.
My shirts are in the closet.
Their car is old.
Their cars are old.

Possessive pronouns

Possessive pronouns also show that something belongs to someone. Use a possessive pronoun *without* a noun.

His family lives in Caracas and *mine* lives in Tokyo.
This is my car. That is *hers*.

Object pronouns

Use an object pronoun as the object of a verb or the object of a preposition.

She met *him* at a party last month.
I bought a birthday present for *her*.

Reflexive pronouns

When you look in the mirror, you see a reflection. A mirror reflects. Reflexive pronouns reflect on the subject of the sentence.

You see *yourself* in a mirror.
The child cut *herself* by accident.
I do not need any help. I can do it by *myself*.

PREPOSITIONS

These are the most common prepositions:

about	by	on
above	down	over
across	during	since
after	for	through
along	from	to
around	in	toward
at	into	under
before	in back of	until
behind	in front of	up
below	near	with
beside	of	without
between	off	

On

on = touching something
    over and touching something

The dish is *on* the table.
The clock is *on* the wall.

Use *on* in some time expressions.

on Tuesday (days)
on April 20 (dates)
on Sunday afternoon
on a street (on Apple Street)   on weekends
on my vacation   on time
on the way   go on a tour
on the weekend   lie on the beach

To

To shows movement.

My sister goes *to* work at 8:00 a.m.
I walked *to* the bus stop.
go to class
go to school
go to work

BUT:

go downtown   go skating
go home   go sightseeing
go shopping   go swimming
write to someone

At

At shows place (location).

Please meet me *at* the Student Union at 6:00.
She had dinner *at* a restaurant last night.

Use *at* with some time expressions.

at 6:00; at 7:14 (exact time)
at night
at noon
at midnight
at a restaurant
at an address
at the beach
at home
arrive at   (But: arrive home, arrive in a city)
late at night

By

by = near, next to

The chair is *by* the window.

by = along, through, past

We took a walk *by* the river.   (along, or beside it).
We entered the house *by* the side door.
We drove *by* the new shopping center.   (We did not stop there or go in. We drove past it.)

by + V-ing tells how to do something. It answers the question, "How?"

David learned to play the guitar *by practicing* every day.
(How did David learn to play the guitar?)
Pierre found out the answer *by asking* a classmate.
(How did Pierre find out the answer?)

by 6:00 = before 6:00 or at 6:00 but not after 6:00

For

for dinner
leave for

For/since

We often use *for* and *since* with the present perfect tense. Use *for* for a period of time. Use *since* for a point in time such as a day, date, month, or year.

Ali has been here *for* six months.
He has been here *since* January.
He has studied English *since* he was a child.

From . . . to

Use *from . . . to* for time and places.

We were in Canada *from* July 1 *to* August 15.
We drove *from* Barcelona *to* Madrid.

In

In shows that something is inside something else.

My class is *in* the Modern Languages Building.
The clothes are *in* the closet.

Use *in* with geographical names.

in a city (in Montreal)	in a country (in Brazil)
in a state (in Kansas)	in a continent (in Europe)

Use *in* with some time expressions.

in the morning	in August (month)
in the afternoon	in summer (season)
in the evening	in 1985 (year)

Use *in* for some future time expression.

They are going to visit Japan in three weeks.
  (three weeks from now)
Tom is going to enter college in two months.
  (two months from now)
in a hurry
in the mountains
in three days (three days from now)
arrive in a city (BUT: arrive at the university/airport/bus station, arrive home)

Preposition + V-ing (prep + N, prep + V-ing)

A preposition usually has a noun or *V-ing* after it. The *V-ing* is the noun form of the verb. When we use *V-ing* as a noun, we call it a *gerund*. (*To* is different because it often has the simple verb after it. There are also some two-word verbs that must have a simple verb instead of a gerund.)

I am thinking *about buying* a new car.
She is interested *in studying* chemistry.
We are going to stay here instead *of flying* to Europe.
You can improve your English *by watching* television.
We use a stove *for cooking*.
I look forward *to seeing* you.

ADVERBS OF FREQUENCY

These are adverbs of frequency: *always, usually, often, sometimes, seldom, rarely, never*

Present tense

Put these words after the verb *be*.

She is *always* late for class.
We are *never* busy on Sunday.

Put these words before other verbs.

I *usually* get up at 7:00 a.m.
My brother *often* goes shopping in the evening.

Negatives

Use *not* with *always, usually,* and *often*. Do not use it with *sometimes, seldom, rarely,* or *never*. Write (*do/does*) *not* before the adverb of frequency.

Ruth *does not* usually get up early on Saturday.
I am *not* usually busy on Saturday.
He *never* studies on Saturday night.

Questions

Put *always* or *usually* after the subject in a question.

Does he *always* talk a lot?
Are you *usually* home on Sunday?

Often is usually at the end of a question.

Do you go there *often*?

We do not usually use *sometimes, seldom, rarely,* or *never* in questions.
We often use *ever* in a question. The question means the same without *ever*.

Does she ride her bicycle to school?
Does she *ever* ride her bicycle to school?

Put *always, usually,* or *ever* after *is/are there*.

Is there *usually* a quiz on Friday?

Present continuous

Do not use adverbs of frequency with the present continuous tense.

Present perfect

Put the adverb of frequency between *have/has* and the past participle.

She *has never been* to France.

Questions

Put the adverb of frequency after the subject in a question. We often use *ever* in present perfect questions.

Have you *always* lived in a big house?
Have you *ever* been to France?

With Modals

Put the adverb of frequency after the modal.

You must *never* do that again.

Negatives

Put the adverb of indefinite frequency after *not*.

I cannot *always* take you to the university in my car.

Questions

Put the adverb of frequency after the subject in a question. We often use *ever* in questions.

Will you *ever* learn to write perfect compositions?

VERY/TOO

Very makes an adjective stronger.

The weather was hot.
The weather was *very* hot.
We live in an old house.
We live in a *very* old house.

Too means *too much*. It gives the sentence a negative feeling or idea. We often write *to* and a simple verb after a *too* phrase.

The weather was *too cold to go swimming*.
(We could not go swimming.)
Our daughter is *too young to drive*.
(She cannot drive.)
Ann was *too tired to go out* in the evening.
(She did not go out.)

ADVERBIALS OF PURPOSE

Sometimes we answer the question *why* with the answer *because* ... We can also use an adverbial of purpose. Use *to* and a verb or *for* and a noun.

Why is Masako studying tonight?
She is studying *because* she has a test tomorrow.
She is studying *to pass* a test tomorrow.
She is studying *for a test* tomorrow.

ALREADY/YET

We often use *already* and *yet* with the present perfect. Use *already* with an affirmative sentence and *yet* with a negative sentence. Use either *already* or *yet* in questions. Put *yet* at the end of the sentence. Put *already* between *have/has* and the present participle or at the end of the sentence.

Summary

already	*yet*
affirmative *have* + *already* + past part. questions	negative (sentence) *yet*. questions

Marie has been in Montreal for a month. She has *already* visited Quebec and Ottawa. She has not been to Toronto *yet*. She plans to go soon.

Already shows that something has happened. *Yet* shows that something has not happened but possibly will happen.

FOR/SINCE

We often use *for* and *since* with the present perfect tense. Use *for* for a period of time. Use *since* for a point in time such as a day, date, month, or year.

Ali has been here *for* six months.
He has been here *since* January.
He has studied English *since* he was a child.

DEMONSTRATIVES

	Singular	Plural
Here	this	these
There	that	those

This student with me is from Malaysia.
These students with me are from Malaysia.
That student over there is from Kuwait.
Those students over there are from Kuwait.

QUESTIONS

There are two kinds of questions in English. The names come from the answers you expect.

1. Yes/no questions
    You expect *yes* or *no* as the answer.

    > Is her name Mary? Yes. (No.)
    > Do you live in a dormitory? Yes. (No.)

2. Wh- or information questions
    You expect some information as the answer. Most question words begin with wh-: who, what, where, why, when, how

    > Her name is Mary.
    > Is her name Mary? (Yes.)

    What is her name? (Mary.)

    Who is that? (David Brown)
    What is your name? (Mary Davis)
    Where is the post office? (next to the bank)
    Why are you studying English? (I need it for my job.)
    When do you usually arrive at the university? (at 8:30)
    How far is it to Chicago? (250 miles)

3. *How* + adjective

how much	how long	how old
how many	how far	how big

    I have twenty dollars with me.
    How much money do you have with you?

    I have two brothers and a sister.
    How many brothers and sisters do you have?

    It is fifteen blocks to the immigration office.
    How far is it to the immigration office?

    I am twenty-one years old.
    How old are you?

    Mexico City has a population of sixteen million.
    How big is Mexico City?

    Tom has lived here for three years.
    How long has Tom lived here?

USEFUL TIME EXPRESSIONS

yesterday	today	tomorrow
yesterday morning	this morning	tomorrow morning
yesterday afternoon	this afternoon	tomorrow afternoon
last night	tonight	tomorrow night
last week	this week	next week
last month	this month	next month

last year	this year	next year
last summer	this summer	next summer
last vacation	this vacation	next vacation
the day before yesterday		the day after tomorrow
two minutes ago		in two minutes
three hours ago		in three hours
four days ago		in four days
five weeks ago		in five weeks
six months ago		in six months
seven years ago		in seven years

SPELLING

Plural nouns

1. Most plural nouns end in *-s*.

room – rooms	tree – trees
car – cars	house – houses

2. Add *-es* to a noun that ends in *s, ch, sh,* or *x*.

bus – buses	dish – dishes
church – churches	box – boxes

3. If a noun ends in *y* and there is a consonant before the *y*, change the *y* to *i* and add *-es*.

baby – babies	lady – ladies

4. If a noun ends in *y* and there is a vowel before the *y*, add *-s*.

boy – boys	day – days

5. If a noun ends in *f*, change the *f* to *v* and add *-es*. If a noun ends in *fe*, change the *f* to *v* and add *-s*.

leaf – leaves	wife – wives

6. Some nouns are irregular. Memorize them.

foot – feet	man – men
tooth – teeth	woman – women
sheep – sheep	child – children

Summary

Singular	Plural
most nouns	*-s*
-s *-ch* *-sh* *-x*	*-es*
consonant *-y* vowel *-y*	*-ies* *-ys*
-f *-fe*	*-ves*

-s form of verbs

The rules for adding -s to verbs are the same as the rules for adding -s to nouns.

1. Add -s to the simple form of most verbs for the third person singular.

   eat – eats   get – gets   like – likes

2. If a verb ends in s, ch, sh, or x add -es.

   pass – passes   finish – finishes
   teach – teaches   box – boxes

3. If a verb ends in y and there is a consonant before the y, change the y to i and add -es.

   study – studies   try – tries

4. If a verb ends in y and there is a vowel before the y, just add -s.

   play – plays   enjoy – enjoys

5. *Do* and *go* are irregular.

   do – does   go – goes

Past tense

1. Add -ed to most regular verbs.

   walk – walked   brush – brushed

2. If the verb ends in -e, just add -d.

   live – lived   use – used

3. If a verb ends in -y and there is a consonant before the -y, change the y to i and add -ed.

   study – studied   carry – carried

4. If a verb ends in -y and there is a vowel before the -y, just add -ed.

   play – played   stay – stayed

5. If a verb has one syllable with one vowel followed by one consonant, double the consonant and add -ed. This is the one-one-one rule (1–1–1).

   shop – shopped   BUT: help – helped
   plan – planned   clean – cleaned

Verb-ing

1. If a verb ends in -e, drop the e and add -ing.

   write – writing   leave – leaving

2. If a verb has one syllable with one vowel followed by one consonant, double the consonant and add -ing (1–1–1 rule).

   shop – shopping   plan – planning

3. If a one-syllable word ends in -ie, change the -ie to -y and add -ing.

   lie – lying   tie – tying

4. Do not change a verb that ends in -y.

   study – studying   hurry – hurrying

Comparisons of adjectives

1. If an adjective ends in -y and there is a consonant before the -y, change the y to i and add -er or -est.

pretty – prettier – prettiest
easy – easier – easiest

2. If an adjective has one syllable with one vowel followed by one consonant, double the consonant and add *-er* or *-est* (the 1–1–1 rule).

    big – bigger – biggest   fat – fatter – fattest

CAPITAL LETTERS

Use capital letters on:

1.	the first word in a sentence	He likes to play soccer.
2.	the name of a person	Helen, David, Mary
3.	a nationality or language	Mexican, Canadian, Spanish, English
4.	the name of a day or month	Sunday, Wednesday, August, October
5.	(The names of seasons do *not* begin with a capital letter.)	spring, summer, fall, winter
6.	titles of people	Ms. Brown, Dr. Collins
7.	the name of a street	Main Street, Park Avenue, Rosewood Boulevard
8.	the names of cities, states, countries, and continents	New York, California, Canada, Asia
9.	other geographical names	the Pacific Ocean, the Amazon River, Mount Everest, Lake Geneva
10.	the names of buildings	the Student Union, the Chemistry Building
11.	the names of holidays	Independence Day, National Day, Ramadan
12.	religious words	Buddha, Islam, the Bible

Titles

Most words in titles have capital letters. Rules:

1. Always use a capital letter on the first word of a title.
2. Use a capital letter on all the important words.
3. *Do not* use a capital letter on

    a. prepositions (*in, on, of, for, at, between, after*)
    b. connecting words (*and, but, or*)
    c. articles (*a, an, the*)

COMBINING SENTENCES

Method 1

I got up. I took a shower.
I got up *and* took a shower.

He had lunch. He rested for an hour.
He had lunch *and* rested for an hour.

The sentence has one subject and two verbs.

Method 2

I tried to call you last night. The line was busy.
I tried to call you last night *but* the line was busy.
We wanted to eat at the student cafeteria. It was closed.
We wanted to eat at the student cafeteria *but* it was closed.

Each part of the sentence must have a subject and a verb. There is a subject and verb before *but* and a subject and verb after *but*.

Method 3a

Gina is from Italy. Tony is from Italy.
Gina *is* from Italy *and* Tony *is too*.
Bob likes to play soccer. Carlos likes to play soccer.
Bob *likes* to play soccer and Carlos *does too*.
Yoko can speak English. Ali can speak English.
Yoko *can* speak English and Ali *can too*.

Method 3b

Ali is studying English. Albert is studying English.
Ali *is* studying English *and* Albert *is too*.

Method 4a

Alice was not at the party last night.
Bob was not at the party last night.
Alice *was not* at the party last night *and* Bob *was not either*.
Betty does not usually eat at home.
Pam does not usually eat at home.
Betty *does not* usually eat at home *and* Pam *does not either*.
Tom cannot drive. Pat cannot drive.
Tom *cannot* drive and Pat *cannot either*.

Method 4b

Helen is not living in a dormitory this year.
Betty is not living in a dormitory this year.
Helen *is not* living in a dormitory this year *and* Betty *is not either*.

Method 5a

Robert is not very quiet. Tom is very quiet.
Robert *is not* very quiet *but* Tom *is*.

Ann goes home every weekend. Pat does not go home every weekend.
Ann *goes* home every weekend *but* Pat *does not.*
Jean cannot sing well. Charles can sing well.
Jean *cannot* sing well *but* Charles *can.*

Method 5b

The new students are taking a placement test now.
The continuing students are not taking a placement test now.
The new students *are* taking a placement test now *but* the continuing students *are not.*

Method 6

I have to clean my apartment. I am going to have a party.
I have to clean my apartment *because* I am going to have a party.

Because shows the reason or purpose. It answers the question, "Why?" Write a subject and verb before *because* and a subject and verb after *because.* Do not begin a sentence with *because.* You will learn how to do that later.

Method 7

      A   **B**
I have breakfast. I brush my teeth.
      A   **B**
After I have breakfast, I brush my teeth.
      B   **A**
Or: I brush my teeth after I have breakfast.
      A   **B**
I did my laundry. I went to a friend's apartment.
      A   **B**
After I did my laundry, I went to a friend's apartment.
      B   **A**
Or: I went to a friend's apartment after I did my laundry.

Method 8

      A   **B**
I made some coffee. I got dressed.
      B   **A**
Before I got dressed, I made some coffee.
      A   **B**
Or: I made some coffee before I got dressed.
      A   **B**
I wrote a letter. I went to bed.
      B   **A**
Before I went to bed, I wrote a letter.

A   B
Or: I wrote a letter before I went to bed.

Put *after* with sentence A. (Sentence A happens first.) Put *before* with sentence B. (*after A, before B*)

Method 9

        Mary was six. She started school.
        When Mary was six, she started school.
Or: Mary started school *when* she was six.

Put the person's name in the first part of the sentence.

Method 10

The phone rang *while* I *was eating* dinner.
I was eating dinner *when* the phone *rang*.
I interrupted him *while* he *was studying*.
He was studying *when* I *interrupted* him.

We often use *while* or *when* to combine a past tense sentence and a past continuous sentence. *While* is always with the past continuous part of the sentence. *When* is always with the past tense part of the sentence. This kind of sentence shows that one action interrupted another action.

Method 11

I will give you the book tonight.
I will see you tonight.
I *will give* you the book *when* I *see* you tonight.
She is going to study the verbs.
She will know them.
She *is going to study* the verbs *until* she *knows* them.
He will get a master's degree.
He will start looking for a job.
He *will get* a master's degree *before* he *starts* looking for a job.
I will finish my English course.
I will start on my Ph.D.
I *will start* on my Ph.D. after I *finish* my English course.
The sentence with *when, until, before,* or *after* is in the present tense even when the real time is future.

WRITING GOOD SENTENCES

1. Every sentence must have a subject and a verb. (Imperatives do not have a subject.)
2. Some sentences have a direct object (D.O.). The direct object is directly after the verb. There is nothing between the verb and the direct object. The direct object is usually a noun. Sometimes the noun has an adjective

or an article (*a, an, the*). The direct object answers the question "What?" or "Who?"

        S   V   D.O.
Jim usually has a big sandwich for lunch.
Jim usually has   <u>what?</u>   for lunch. (a big sandwich)

        S   V   D.O.
I often visit John on Sunday.
I often visit   <u>who(m)?</u>   on Sunday. (John)

3. We often write a list of three or more things in a sentence. Separate the things in the list with commas. Write *and* or *or* before the last thing in the list.

> In the morning I get up, take a shower, comb my hair, and brush my teeth.
> I usually have coffee, toast, and eggs for breakfast.
> I have lunch in the cafeteria, in a restaurant, or at home.
> My parents, my sisters, and my brother all live in Toronto.

4. A phrase is a group of words but it is not a sentence.
A prepositional phrase has a preposition and an object. The object is usually a noun. A prepositional phrase sometimes has an article (*a, an, the*) or an adjective too.
These are some prepositional phrases:

for dinner	after dinner	after my last class
in the morning	on Saturday	on Sunday afternoon

Put some prepositional phrases at the end of the sentence. Put some at the beginning. This makes the composition more interesting.
Example:

> John leaves for class *at 8:00*. He has classes and studies in the library *until noon. In the afternoon* he has two classes. *After his last class* he goes home. He does his homework and watches television *in the evening*.

5. Never connect two sentences with a comma.

    WRONG: She is short, she has black hair.
    RIGHT: She is short. She has black hair.
    WRONG: David is from Mexico, he speaks Spanish.
    RIGHT: David is from Mexico and he speaks Spanish.

WRITING GOOD COMPOSITIONS

1. Every composition must have a title. See page 168 for the rules for putting capital letters on titles.

2. A good composition has an introductory sentence. The introductory sentence introduces the composition to the reader. It is a sentence about the general idea of the composition. A composition should also have a concluding sentence. This is another sentence about the general idea of the composition.

Examples:

MY CAR

I have a Honda Civic car. It is white with a blue interior. It is small but very comfortable. It is easy to drive and it does not use very much gas. *I am glad I have this kind of car.*

MY CLASSROOM

My classroom is on the first floor of a new building. It is a small room with bright yellow walls and two windows. In the front of the room there is a green chalkboard.

My writing class is small and the students all sit around a large table. The chairs are different colors. They are made of plastic and are very comfortable. *My classroom is a pleasant place to study English.*

3. A composition is about only one subject or idea. Every sentence is about the same subject. Look at each example. The sentences in italics are not good sentences for the paragraphs because they are about different subjects. They do not belong in the composition.

I am always very busy during the week. I get up at 7:00 and leave for the university at 7:45. *My university is beautiful and has modern buildings.* I have classes or study until 4:00 and then I go home. I relax for a while, have dinner, and study some more. Then I watch television and go to bed. I am usually tired after a busy day.

María is one of my classmates. She is from Colombia and speaks Spanish. *Bogota is the capital of Colombia.* María is tall and pretty. She smiles a lot and is an excellent student.

4. When you write a composition, put the sentences in a logical, sensible order. In the poor paragraph the sentences are not in the right order. In the second paragraph the sentences are organized correctly.

A poor paragraph:

MY APARTMENT

My apartment is in Mexico City. It is small but it is beautiful. It is on the seventh floor of a large building. There are two bathrooms. There is a kitchen. There is a living room. There is a beautiful view from the balcony. There are a lot of plants in the rooms. There is a dining room. There are three bedrooms. There are a lot of pictures. It is comfortable. There are a lot of windows. I like living in this apartment.

A good composition:

MY APARTMENT

My apartment is in Mexico City. It is small but it is beautiful and comfortable. It is on the seventh floor of a large building and there is a beautiful view from the balcony. There are three bedrooms, a living room, a dining room, a kitchen, and two bathrooms. There are a lot of plants, pictures and windows. I like living in this apartment.

5. Use *Then, Next, After that,* or *and then* to connect ideas. Begin a sentence with *Then, Next,* or *After that.* Use *and then* to connect two sentences into one sentence. Do not use a capital letter on *and then.*

I usually start to study at 4:00. I get my books, notebook, and pencil. *Then* I put them all on my desk. I look at my assignment notes *and then* I find the right page. *Next* I read the directions carefully. *After that* I take a sheet of paper and put my name on it. *Then* I start to do my homework.

LETTER FORM

```
                                    (your address)
                                    2836 E. Speedway, Apt. 6
                                    Tucson, Arizona 85719
                                    December 9, 19__


  Dear _____,


              (body of the letter)




              Your friend,
              (your name)
```

Other closings: Your cousin,
                   Your brother,
                   Yours truly,
                   Sincerely yours,

CHART OF LESSONS

Lesson	Title	Main Structure	Grammar and Usage	Useful Expressions	Mechanics and Style	Review
1	Myself p. 1	present	(diagnostic) none	none	none	none
2	An Interview p. 3	present 3rd pers. sing.	3rd pers. sing. is, has	*be* + age, *like to* + SV	caps: person, sentence, language, nationality, day, month, not seasons, word order for adj. + *hair*	none
3	A Person I Like p. 7	3rd pers. sing.	3rd pers. sing., sentence must have S + V	*at* with time/night, in the morning/ afternoon	comma splice, introductory and concluding sentences	*be* + age, *like to*, 3rd pers. sing.
4	My Daily Activities p. 11	present	present	have food/drink, go home, at home, go to bed, go to sleep, leave for the university, leave for home, arrive at, do homework, watch TV, listen to, go to a movie, go to the movies	caps in titles, *for lunch* at end of sentence, connecting ideas: *then, and then, next, after that*	none
5	My Home p. 17	*there is/are*	*there is/are* adj. before N, no pl. for adj., S + V + D.O.	none	one subject in a composition, spelling: pl N: *-s, -es, -ies, -ve,* irreg.	introductory sentence
6	Yesterday p. 23	past affirmative	past count/ noncount, irregular verbs	go to class/work/ school, go downtown/ shopping/ swimming/skiing, yesterday morning/ afternoon, last night	spelling: *-ied, shopped,* combining sentences: predicates (Method 1)	connecting ideas, useful expres- sions, S + V + D.O.
7	Right Now p. 29	pres. continuous	pres. continu- ous, demon- stratives, *a/an*		spelling: V-ing— *writing, planning, lying, studying,* prep. phrase at beginning of sentence	present, comma splice, spelling: pl N
8	Habitual Actions p. 35	3rd pers. sing. affirmative negative	3rd pers. sing., pres. neg., adv. of frequency, *the*	none	spelling: verb + *-s, -es, -ies, -ys* list in a sentence: ___, ___, and ___	useful expres- sions, caps on title, errors

Lesson	Title	Main Structure	Grammar and Usage	Useful Expressions	Mechanics and Style	Review
9	A Good Day/ A Bad Day p. 41	past neg.	past negative, irreg. verbs, possessive adj.	prep.: *at*	combine: *but* (Method 2)	irreg. verbs, one subj. in a paragraph, *a/the*
10	Two People p. 47	comparisons: adj.	compare: *-er, more, better, worse some/any*	prep: *to*	combine: *and ... too/and ... either/but with be/*other verbs/ *can* (Methods 3, 4, 5) Spelling: *-er*	caps verb + s errors
11	Next Weekend p. 53	*going to:* affirm. neg.	*going to ago/in 3 days* possessive pron.	prep: *in* tomorrow night, next week/ month/year/ summer/vacation, in 1990/June/3 days/5 years	combine: *because* (Method 6)	compare: *-er, most,* possessive adj., errors
12	A Letter to a Friend p. 59	modals, imperatives	modals, imperatives	prep.: *on* be sure to + V, do your best, on time, first of all, look forward to + N/V-ing	possessive nouns	verb tenses, adv. of frequency, errors
13	My City p. 67	comparisons	comparisons: *-est, most, best, worst many/ much/a lot of*	preps: *by = near, along, past* in city, on street, at address, the cost of living, high-rise buildings, rush hour, heavy traffic, a traffic jam	spelling: *-est,* organizing a paragraph	compare: *-er,* articles, errors
14	Weekends p. 73	pres. 3rd pers. sing.	3rd pers. sing., neg., adv. of frequency, questions: affirm., pres./yes– no/wh-, obj. pron.	on weekends, on the weekend, on Sundays, on Sunday afternoon, at a restaurant, have a party, have a picnic	combine: *after* I ... I ...; *before* I ... I ... (Methods 7, 8)	adv. of frequency, spell: verb + s, possessive adj. & pron.
15	A Vacation p. 79	past questions	past questions, irreg. verbs, count noun with *one of/ several/ different/ numbers/a lot of/most of/some of*	prep: *from ... to* visit a place, on my vacation, late at night, stay up, spend time, to get to someplace, spend a vacation	none	past irreg. verbs, past affirm./ neg., errors

Lesson	Title	Main Structure	Grammar and Usage	Useful Expressions	Mechanics and Style	Review
16	Another Letter p. 84	pres. continuous neg. & questions	pres. continuous neg. & questions *very/too*	prep: by *plane*, etc. wait for, buy something for someone, do something for someone, write a letter to someone, board a plane, a plane lands/takes off	combine: *and . . . too, and . . . either, but* with pres. continuous (Methods 3b, 4b, 5b)	spelling: *-ing*, pres. continuous, *and . . . too*, etc.
17	Usually/ Today p. 91	pres. vs. pres. continuous	pres. vs. pres. continuous, verb + *to* + verb	wear/put on/get dressed/a dress, like to vs. would like to	none	count/ noncount, organize a paragraph, errors
18	Since My Arrival p. 96	pres. perf.	past participle (reg. & irreg.) pres. perf. *for/since*	have been to, to tour, go on a tour, take a trip, go sightseeing, arrive in a city	none	past verb forms, *some/any*, errors
19	A Biography p. 101	all tenses	*used to*, irreg. verbs	prep: *by* + V-ing on May 5, in May/1970, start/ enter/attend/go to school, take/pass a test, make friends, grow up, get married	combine: when (Method 9)	verb tenses, irreg. verbs, combine: *before/ after*
20	A Childhood Experi-ence p. 107	past continuous vs. past	past continu-ous: affirm./ neg./ questions, *can/could*, irreg. verbs	think about, each other, get ready, on the way, by 6:00/this p.m./ Thurs./next week	combine: while vs. when (Method 10)	irreg. verbs, all pronouns, pres. continu-ous: neg./ questions
21	Another Interview p. 112	pres. perf.: neg. & questions	pres. perf. irreg. verbs *already/ yet how much/ many/big/ long far/ old*	none	none	poss. nouns pres. perf. irreg. verbs
22	Future Plans p. 118	*will*	*will*: affirm./ neg./ questions	none	combine: will/going to + when/until/ before/after + present (Method 11)	irreg. verbs, *much/ many/a lot of*, rewrite: caps & punctua-tion

Lesson	Title	Main Structure	Grammar and Usage	Useful Expressions	Mechanics and Style	Review
23	Giving Advice p. 123	modals, imperatives	modals: neg./ questions, imperatives: neg., *one/ another one/the other one/ the other ones* adv. of purpose: *go to buy/ go for +* N	none	capitalize & punctuate a paragraph	modals, imperatives, comparisons
24	A Special Vacation p. 129	modals, adv. of freq.	adv. of frequency with modals/ pres. perf., *ever another/ the other/ the others*	none	capitalize & punctuate a paragraph	modals, adv. of frequency, errors
25	A Letter to Myself p. 134	Review	irreg. verbs, reflex pron.	*interested in* + N/ V-ing, old friends, after all, change your mind, instead of, be in a hurry, make a mistake, by proud of, prep. + V-ing/N	none	*used to, very/too,* errors